SpringerBriefs in Regional Science

SpringerBriefs present concise summaries of cutting-edge research and practical applications across a wide spectrum of fields. Featuring compact, authored volumes of 50 to 125 pages, the series covers a range of content from professional to academic. SpringerBriefs in Regional Science showcase emerging theory, empirical research and practical application, lecture notes and reviews in spatial and regional science from a global author community.

All titles in this book series are peer-reviewed. This series is indexed in SCOPUS.

Indraneel Kumar • Roberto Gallardo
Editors

Economic Competitiveness

A Literature Review of Clusters, Innovation and Networks

Springer

Editors
Indraneel Kumar
Purdue Center for Regional Development
Purdue University
West Lafayette, IN, USA

Roberto Gallardo
Office of Engagement and Department of Agricultural Economics
Purdue University
West Lafayette, IN, USA

ISSN 2192-0427 ISSN 2192-0435 (electronic)
SpringerBriefs in Regional Science
ISBN 978-3-032-20358-8 ISBN 978-3-032-20359-5 (eBook)
https://doi.org/10.1007/978-3-032-20359-5

This Springer imprint is published by the registered company Springer Nature Switzerland AG.
The registered company address is: Gewerbestrasse 11, 6330 Cham, Switzerland

Acknowledgments The chapters are modified from a previous version of the literature review prepared by authors using Federal funds under award # ED23RNA0G0174 from the Economic Development Administration, U.S. Department of Commerce, and published here, https://pcrd.purdue.edu/wp-content/uploads/2025/04/Literature-Review_04-21-2025.pdf. The statements, findings, conclusions, and recommendations are those of the author(s) and do not necessarily reflect the views of the Economic Development Administration or the U.S. Department of Commerce. Used with permission.

Contents

Editors and Contributors

About the Editors

Indraneel Kumar is Director of the Purdue Center for Regional Development. He works on regional economic and workforce analysis, demographics, identification of new data sources, spatial analysis, and quantitative methods. He has degrees in architecture, planning, and a Ph.D. in civil engineering, and has led or participated in multiple federal- and state-funded projects. Purdue Center for Regional Development, Purdue University, ikumar@purdue.edu.

Roberto Gallardo is Vice President for Engagement and an Associate Professor in the Agricultural Economics Department. He holds an electronics engineering undergraduate degree, a master's degree in economic development, and a Ph.D. in public policy and administration. Gallardo has worked with rural communities over the past decade conducting local & regional community economic development, including the use of technology for development. Office of Engagement and Department of Agricultural Economics, Purdue University, robertog@purdue.edu.

About the Contributors

Hyewon Shin is Engagement Specialist at Purdue Regional Center for Development (PCRD). She holds a Master's degree in Public Administration from the University of Arizona. Hyewon is working on PCRD's various projects including industry clusters, housing analysis, comprehensive economic development strategy, and other regional economic and community development efforts.Purdue Center for Regional Development, Purdue University, shin457@purdue.edu.

Cheyanne Geideman is Community Development Extension Educator with Purdue Extension serving Allen County. She holds a B.S. in Visual Communications Design from Purdue and an M.A. in International Community Development from Northwest University. Cheyanne leads broadband and digital divide initiatives, addressing connectivity gaps, digital skills, and community planning statewide. Purdue Extension, Purdue University, cgeidema@purdue.edu.

Mark C. White leads Illinois Extension's Community and Economic Development program and is a Clinical Associate Professor with the Department of Agricultural and Consumer Economics at the University of Illinois Urbana-Champaign. For over two decades, he has helped economic and workforce development practitioners make more informed, data-driven decisions about how to strengthen their regional economies and workforce. Department of Agricultural and Consumer Economics and Illinois Extension, University of Illinois Urbana-Champaign, whitemc@illinois.edu.

Annie Cruz-Porter is a Community and Regional Development Specialist at the Purdue Center for Regional Development (PCRD). She plans and guides the implementation of regional economic strategies intended to enhance the resiliency of regions across Indiana. Annie has a PhD from the University of Sheffield in England. Purdue Center for Regional Development, Purdue University, acruzpor@purdue.edu.

Chapter 1
Introduction

Indraneel Kumar and Roberto Gallardo

Abstract Regional development is a dynamic field. With the rapid digitization of the economy and a highly connected society, updated frameworks are warranted to better understand opportunities and challenges around a classic regional economic development paradigm: industry clusters. This chapter discusses the outline and the rationale to update industry clusters and their relationship with occupations and skills, knowledge and innovation, and social networks.

Keywords Cluster-based economic development · Innovation · Occupation and skills clusters · Network analysis · Industry clusters

As society and the economy continue to digitize and as applications with the potential of general-purpose technologies are adopted by small and large businesses, organizations, government, and residents, the need to revisit cluster-based economic development theory and practice is overdue. This approach to economic development is one of many in a broader regional development literature ranging from theories of regional economic divergence to structuralist theories to emerging neoclassical perspectives (Dawkins, 2003).

These theories attempt to understand how regions grow, why some regions grow more rapidly than others, and why there are regional differences in wealth and social welfare. However, regional development across the United States is very

I. Kumar (✉)
Purdue Center for Regional Development, Purdue University, West Lafayette, IN, USA
e-mail: ikumar@purdue.edu

R. Gallardo
Office of Engagement and Department of Agricultural Economics, Purdue University, West Lafayette, IN, USA
e-mail: robertog@purdue.edu

I. Kumar, R. Gallardo (eds.), *Economic Competitiveness*, SpringerBriefs in Regional Science,
https://doi.org/10.1007/978-3-032-20359-5_1

unequal. Practitioners and scholars alike continue to be nagged at "left behind" or persistently poor regions (Fikri, 2024). Due to this unequal regional development, federal policy emphasizes place-based policies launching programs such as the Build Back Better Regional Challenge,[1] Tech Hubs,[2] Recompete,[3] and Regional Engines.[4]

The role of innovation and talent is also being revisited, particularly due to the advent of digital infrastructure and applications. While the concept of the "death of distance" surfaced back in the late 1990s, it seems to have lost ground ever since, as argued by Moretti in his 2012 "The New Geography of Jobs" book. This too contributes to the unequal regional development across the country.

It is naïve to think that the concept of industry clusters and their increasingly complex relationship with innovation and talent have not been affected by this changing regional and economic landscape. Time and time again, outdated paradigms and inadequate benchmarks become less useful for practitioners, policymakers, and scholars. For these reasons, not only were the definitions of industry clusters revisited, but also the related topics were also reviewed that when woven together provides a refreshed and broader understanding of cluster-based economic development paradigm.

This book is a result of the literature review completed as part of the "Updating Industry Clusters" project funded by the U.S. Economic Development Administration (EDA) during 2024 and 2025. The book presents a comprehensive review of the published research on industry clusters and related topics with the intent to update these definitions and identify new clusters as well as to incorporate the literature and definitions around innovation, occupations and skills clusters, and network analysis. The focus areas of this literature review were informed, in part, by a bibliometric analysis of the literature compiled by using the Web of Science (WoS) and SCOPUS (Elsevier's abstract and citation repository) databases. In addition, the interviews of academicians and practitioners conducted as part of the EDA project informed the subject areas of the literature review. The co-authors of this book and the project team also discussed and refined the topics and subject areas for the literature review.

This book is divided into five chapters, including this introduction. Chapter 2 provides an overview of industry clusters and regional economic competitiveness. Key benchmarks, technical aspects, and methodological nuances are discussed, including types of clusters (traded versus local) and the development of the first traded cluster definitions using locational correlation by Porter (2003). There have been five major efforts to define industry clusters and develop benchmarked cluster

[1] https://www.eda.gov/funding/programs/american-rescue-plan/build-back-better.

[2] Regional Technology and Innovation Hubs, https://www.eda.gov/funding/programs/regional-technology-and-innovation-hubs.

[3] Distressed Areas Recompete Pilot Program, https://www.eda.gov/funding/programs/recompete-pilot-program.

[4] Regional Innovation Engines, https://www.nsf.gov/funding/initiatives/regional-innovation-engines.

definitions for the United States in the past, since 2000. The chapter provides succinct descriptions of the previous research efforts.

Chapter 3 explores the economic geography of knowledge and innovation by reviewing literature from the United States and international contexts. The review concentrates on the development and dissemination of new knowledge and innovations related to industry clusters. It delves into diffusion and sharing of codified versus tacit or explicit versus implicit knowledge within and between the industry clusters. This section introduces and explains terms, such as epistemic communities and local knowledge spillovers. The chapter ends with several international case studies of industry clusters and how clusters are considered for regional economic development in other countries.

Chapter 4 explores occupations and skills clusters and how they can add invaluable insights into human capital for public programs, private investments, and educational institutes within the regions. The review presents the need for new data sources and analytical methods to understand the linkages between occupations and skills and crosswalks to the industries. Occupations and skills have often been overlooked and not integrated into industry clusters, creating a significant blind spot for practitioners.

Chapter 5, the final section, reviews the theories of social networks, social capital, and network analysis. The review looks at the role of networks and interactions and information flows in industry cluster development and the role of network analysis in uncovering these relationships. Furthermore, it provides a useful epistemology to understand how elements within a cluster interact. Before social networks and network analysis, it was obvious, but not entirely understood, how cooperation within industries in a cluster resulted in innovation and competitive advantage.

This book explores the topic of regional competitiveness from different but important lenses, which include agglomeration and production of goods and services; human capital or occupations and skills present in the regions; discovery and dissemination of knowledge and innovation in regional economies; and the role of social networks and culture in regional economic competitiveness.

The review provides evidence that the expectations from industry cluster analysis have changed over the decades.

During the late 1990s, 2000s, and 2010s, the purpose of industry cluster analysis was to identify competitive industry clusters and sectors for regions and develop economic development strategies to promote the competitive industry clusters and sectors. The emphasis was on metrics such as job growth, reducing unemployment rate, and wages. Whereas these metrics remain important, the industry cluster concept is embracing new paradigms such as resilience, ecosystems, and human capital development. For example, an overarching and integrated cluster is an entirely new lens to view economic resilience and competitiveness.

The boundaries between traditional fields of economic, community, and workforce development have merged. For practitioners and researchers, occupation clusters are as important as the industry clusters. The advent of artificial intelligence (AI) and high technological areas has incited the importance and interest in skill development focusing on growing, attracting, and retaining talent in the region. In addition, the advent of AI may affect the innovation process as it is understood today. There is an opportunity for further research on occupations and skills clusters and interrelationships between industries, occupations, knowledge, skills, and networks.

Similarly, social networks present significant opportunities for research in the areas of industry and occupation clusters, workforce development, and human capital. Another potential area of research is related to data applications including methods to uncover detailed industry-to-industry transactions or flow data to facilitate research on economic networks.

This book lays the foundation for updated industry cluster definitions and their relationship with occupations and skills, innovation, and social networks. These definitions and interrelationships better reflect the current regional economic development landscape. Collectively, this book should provide not only an updated lens to understand regional development and hopefully help address its persistent challenges, but also more useful benchmarks and tools for practitioners and scholars alike.

References

Dawkins, C. (2003). Regional development theory: Conceptual foundations, classic works, and recent development. *Journal of Planning Literature*, *18*(2), 131–172. https://doi.org/10.1177/0885412203254706

Fikri, K. (2024). Persistently poor, left-behind and chronically disconnected. *Cambridge Journal of Regions, Economy, and Society*, *17*(1), 249–258. https://doi.org/10.1093/cjres/rsad048

Moretti, E. (2012). *The new geography of jobs*. Houghton Mifflin Harcourt.

Porter, M. (2003). The economic performance of regions. *Regional Studies*, *37*(6–7), 549–578.

Chapter 2
Industry Clusters and Regional Economic Competitiveness

Indraneel Kumar

Abstract This chapter explores the origins and evolution of the industry cluster concept with a focus on the efforts undertaken in the United States. It presents the different scholarly perspectives on the concept of agglomeration and provides details of the specific U.S.-based initiatives on developing and using the benchmark industry clusters for regional economic development purposes. In addition, variants such as knowledge-based and integrated industry clusters are discussed, including the data limitations. The chapter concludes with a summary and briefly describes new avenues of research on agglomeration, competitiveness, and clusters.

Keywords Regional economic competitiveness · Agglomeration · Marshall–Arrow–Romer · Input–output analysis · Knowledge-based industry clusters

This chapter explores the origins of industry clusters as a framework for regional economic development and competitiveness. It traces the advent of the agglomeration concept, the evolution of the industry cluster framework, major projects undertaken in the United States, and the methods to delineate the industry cluster definitions. The chapter concludes with introducing the emerging areas of research related to industry clusters and regional economic competitiveness.

I. Kumar (✉)
Purdue Center for Regional Development, Purdue University, West Lafayette, IN, USA
e-mail: ikumar@purdue.edu

I. Kumar, R. Gallardo (eds.), *Economic Competitiveness*, SpringerBriefs in Regional Science,
https://doi.org/10.1007/978-3-032-20359-5_2

2.1 Origins of the Industry Clusters

Industry cluster is a commonly applied term in contemporary regional economic development practices in the United States. Academic scholars have debated on the origins of the concept and concluded that the first reference on clustering of industries occurred in *Principles of Economics* authored by Alfred Marshall in the late nineteenth century. Marshall described how specialized industries developed and concentrated in particular locations and how locally available natural and physical resources, human skills, and trade craftsmen prompted the development and growth of economic enterprises attracting supplementary and supporting industries in proximity to each other (Marshall, 1890). In many ways, the concept of modern industry clusters in the United States, which are also known as industrial districts in Europe, refers to the Marshallian principles of benefits from external and internal economies of scale and agglomeration advantages (Kumar et al., 2017).

Kadokawa (2011) researched four Marshallian benefits, which nurture the agglomeration of industries. These included knowledge spillover, skilled labor pool, supporting industries or suppliers, and input resources such as raw materials. In a survey of new industries in Japan, the first set of variables included proximity to related firms, headquarters, and research institutions; support from governments; land prices; co-location with other firms; and availability of water and amenities in the region mattered for new industrial plants (Kadokawa, 2011). The second set of significant variables included proximity to raw materials and markets; business and logistics services; and labor availability and technical skills pointing to the importance of transportation and logistics services (Kadokawa, 2011). The third aspect included social and professional networks such as the variable on manager's personal ties in making the decision to locate in a specific region (Kadokawa, 2011). This research elucidated that in addition to location-specific factors such as access to highways, firms considered Marshallian agglomeration benefits and industrial cluster characteristics in choosing a specific region within the country. The location decisions of firms could be divided into two hierarchical levels: regional and site-level locations. It was at a higher spatial level of regions that opportunities for industrial clustering guided the decisions for locating or creating new industrial plants, and site-specific factors guided the decision to locate in a specific place, such as an industrial park (Kadokawa, 2011).

A reference to agglomeration is incomplete without a discourse on "localization or clustering of similar industries" versus "urbanization or clustering of diverse industries," two noteworthy mechanisms of agglomeration explained by regional economists. There is an ongoing debate among scholars if the regions should strive for specialization of industries versus diversification and variety in industries. According to Cortright (2006), the findings from previous research have been mixed with some studies providing evidence in favor of specialization of industries and some uncovering evidence in favor of diversification of industries.

Ellison and Glaeser (1997) put forth that the expectation of increasing returns is the primary motivation for an industrial plant to select a specific location. The authors consider two types of agglomerative forces causing the increasing returns: physical and intellectual spillovers, and natural advantages such as proximity to water resources (Ellison & Glaeser, 1997). Physical spillovers include transport cost externalities because firms agglomerate to take advantage of economies of scale and save transport costs and create labor demand to attract large numbers of labor force, which eventually results in a positive-feedback cycle as posited by Arthur (1990) and Krugman (1991).[1] The focus of Krugman (1991) was on developing an explanatory but rigorous economic model of why manufacturing in the United States is concentrated in proximate geographies known as "core" with the remaining part of the country and the world known as "periphery" serving the industries located in the "core." While developing the "core-periphery" theory, Krugman (1991) was inspired by the "circular and cumulative causation" model by Myrdal (1957) and the "positive feedback" model by Arthur (1990). In simpler terms, Myrdal's and Arthur's frameworks postulate that specialization begets further specialization causing the rise in labor demand, attracting migrants, and eventually resulting in economic growth and development. An example of "positive feedback" is that the probability an industry may come to a region depends in part on the existing proportion of that industry (specialization) in the region (Arthur, 1990). It is important to note that Myrdal (1957) attempted to provide an explanation of spatial inequities in regional economic development across nations leaning in favor of "divergence" or disequilibrium than "convergence" or equilibrium schools of thoughts. Sheppard (2017) described that "uneven geographical development" (p. 973) was considered by Myrdal as a norm than an exception.

The international trade and the new economic geography theories postulated by Krugman (1991) could explain why diverse countries are specializing and at the same time trading in similar products such as automobiles. However, scholars including Krugman have noted that the manufacturing patterns that inspired the development of the theory have been unraveling especially after the 1990s (Bruilhart, 2009). The manufacturing from the United States and Europe has been dispersing to the developing countries creating specializations in the "periphery" regions in contrast to the original core-periphery pattern assumptions (Bruilhart, 2009). However, after the COVID-19 pandemic, scholars are interested in the wisdom of Krugman's New Economic Geography (NEG) theory to explain spatial economic patterns accounting for frictions such as distances, border restrictions, tariffs, lockdowns, and the push and pull factors reshaping the agglomerations in developed and developing economies (Nijkamp et al., 2024).

[1] Paul Krugman developed the new international trade theory focusing on monopolistic competition and intra-industry trade in the world. For example, Sweden and the United States are both developed economies and produce different brands of automobiles to sell to each other. Consumers benefit from the variety of products in the market.

As scholars in economics and geography attempted to theorize and explain patterns of economic development, a new framework emerged in 1990. In the wide-ranging discourse on means for economic growth and success, *The Competitive Advantage of Nations* by Michael Porter holds a significant landmark. In this treatise, Porter (1990) stated that "national prosperity is created and not inherited," and competition and innovation between industries are the ways to achieve competitive and comparative advantages. In this context, the role of government shall be to enable conditions for competition and innovation without interfering into operations of the firms and industrial processes (Porter, 1990). With increased globalization and faster means of transportation and communication enabling movement from anywhere to anywhere, the dictum of "location, location, and location" should have faded away. However, Porter (1998) uncovered that contrary to losing importance, "locations" became even more important for the success of businesses and industries. Porter (1998) found that competitive advantages were embedded in the select groups of interconnected firms that were highly specialized and competitive but located only in specific locations. These groups of interconnected firms were termed "clusters" by Porter (1998). In fact, industry clusters were recognized as the building blocks of global value chains and competitiveness of the nations. In many ways "clusters" operationalized the concepts of agglomeration, cumulative causation, and positive feedback along with the capacity to explain the spatial disequilibrium and inequities observed between regional economies. It was almost a merger of strands of thinking happening around the contributions of Marshall, Myrdal, and Arthur. The introduction of the industry cluster concept in the late 1990s was a seminal contribution to academic research and professional practice of regional economic development in the United States.

2.2 Defining Benchmark Industry Clusters: Early and Contemporary Efforts in the United States

2.2.1 Early 2000s

The decades of research in economic geography had attempted to explain variations in economic development between regions. Whereas the national framework for economic competitiveness was available, the substantial regional-level differences in the economic growth and development could not be explained properly. In the early 2000s, Michael Porter investigated the role of industry cluster specializations in explaining the economic development and prosperity of the regions (Porter, 2003). It was established that national competitiveness relied on specializations in industry clusters, which were not universal across the nation, but were located in select regions. Porter (2003) used County Business Patterns (CBP)[2] data from 1990 to 2000 based on Standard Industry Classification (SIC) to identify definitions for 41 traded clusters in the United States. Porter (2003) used co-location based on Pearson's correlation coefficients[3] of SIC 4-digit employment at the state level to delineate definitions of industry clusters. After defining the clusters, the data were aggregated for the 172 Economic Areas (EAs)[4] developed by the Bureau of Economic Analysis (BEA). Porter (2003) explored average wages, employment, and compound annual growth rates of wages and employment to describe differences in economic performances between regions. However, the author could not uncover any substantial relationship between initial higher wages and growth rates in wages to explain employment levels or growth in employment and vice versa. After employment and wages, Porter (2003) investigated innovation by using patents and patent intensity[5] to explain the economic performance of regions and study relationships with employment and average wages. The relationships between patent intensity and average wages and employment were found to be significant. The author defined industry clusters by distinguishing between "local" (geographically dispersed) and "traded" (geographically concentrated) types of industries in a regional economy. A third category of "resource dependent" industries such as logging and mining was also identified.

The local industries serving the local population accounted for nearly 67% of total employment, traded industries exporting to other regions and nations accounted for 32% of total employment, and resource-dependent industries accounted for only 1% of the total employment (Porter, 2003). The traded industries exporting goods and services were unique to the regions, but local industries were present proportionately in every region (Porter, 2003). The author distinguished traded industry from local industry if location quotient (LQ)[6] was ≥ 1, industry employment was ≥ 50% of total employment, mean LQ of the top five states was ≥ 2, and employment GINI[7] coefficient was 0.3. In addition to employment patterns, the author also applied knowledge of the industries, definitions of

---

[2] County Business Patterns (CBP) data exclude government and military employment. The CBP is mainly comprised of private sector employment excluding agricultural workers, railroad workers, household employment, self-employed, etc. At the county level, CBP data are highly suppressed.

[3] $r = \sum (X_i - \bar{X})(Y_i - \bar{Y}) / \sqrt{\sum (X_i - \bar{X})^2 \sum (Y_i - \bar{Y})^2}$; where r is Pearson's correlation coefficient, X_i is the X variable, and Y_i is the Y variable.

[4] Economic Areas (EAs) were defined by the Bureau of Economic Analysis (BEA). These were delineations of the regional markets spanning the entire United States. In 2004, BEA increased the number of EAs from 172 to 179 (Johnson & Kort, 2004).

[5] Patents per 100,000 residents and patent per capita.

[6] LQ is known as the location quotient. It is a ratio of employment share of an industry in a region with respect to the nation. $LQ = \frac{R_i}{R_n} / \frac{N_i}{N_n}$, where R is employment in region, N is employment in nation, i is industry, and n is total. LQ ≥ 1 is considered as the cutoff point for specialization or exporting in EBT.

[7] GINI is a measure of inequality. Higher values of GINI coefficient mean more inequality which shows that employment/income/wages are more concentrated in fewer regions.

industries, and judgment to distinguish between local and traded industries. It is to be noted that the data were analyzed for U.S. states to account for data suppression in smaller geographies.

Whereas traded industries accounted for only one-third of employment on average in a region, it could explain average wages and employment growth in regions substantially, facilitating Porter (2003) to develop 41 traded cluster definitions for the first time in the United States. Hence, Porter (2003) can be attributed to developing the first set of the locational correlation (LC) or co-location-based industry cluster definitions for the United States. The author used an iterative approach to distinguish 41 narrowly defined and, to some extent, mutually exclusive (partially overlapping) industry clusters based on statistically significant correlations of employment between traded industry sectors at the state level. The National Input–Output (IO) table was further used to ensure that cluster definitions aligned with the interindustry linkages. In addition, judgment and knowledge of industries were used to exclude highly correlated but unrelated industry pairs from the cluster definitions (Porter, 2003).

The development of industry clusters and related research was a milestone in that it established that specializations in clusters and not in individual industry sectors mattered for the regional economic performance and national competitiveness. Porter (2003) described industry clusters as "geographically proximate group of interconnected companies, suppliers, service providers and associated institutions in a particular field, linked by externalities of various types (p. 562)." For the first time, there was evidence that industries along with their suppliers and associated institutions constituted the relevant framework for regional economic development research, practice, and decision-making.

During the same period, U.S. researchers pursued another strand of thinking around the development of industry cluster definitions. The exploration of this method in developing benchmark industry clusters for the United States can be attributed to Edward Feser and Edward Bergman. Feser and Bergman (2000) delineated industry cluster definitions based on interindustry linkages and hence explored a methodology more quantitative than the descriptive and qualitative approaches undertaken by scholars and practitioners in the previous decades. The authors derived manufacturing value chain clusters for the United States, by using the 1987 National Input–Output (IO), 362 × 362 interindustry data based on the SIC, an older but prevalent industry classification system. The clusters were derived for both manufacturing and nonmanufacturing industry sectors by using the intermediate purchases and sales between industries. It is to be noted that Bergman and Feser (1999) identified IO analysis as one of the key methods to define clusters in addition to the expert opinion, LQ, network analysis, and surveys. However, the origins of IO analysis for identifying clusters or meaningful groupings of industries can be traced back to Czamanski and Ablas (1979) and O'hUallachain (1984). While explaining the value of analyzing flows in identifying industry clusters, Czamanski and Ablas (1979) emphasized that IO-based methods create "aspatial clusters (p. 62)," and the defined clusters were needed to be studied in spatial contexts. Scholars as early as the

1970s identified the value of spatial analysis and mapping of industry clusters, especially in the context of industrial complexes.

The authors argued in favor of benchmark clusters explaining that such definitions and their applications in different regions can uncover unique industrial mixes and compositions in different regions within the same cluster. In so doing, benchmark clusters can reveal unique strengths and weaknesses of the regions including supply chain gaps and opportunities for economic development in the region (Feser & Bergman, 2000). The authors developed purchase and sales coefficients[8] by using the IO transaction values, ran correlations based on four coefficients, selected the largest coefficient, and ran Principal Component Analysis with Varimax rotation to derive factors or industry clusters. Based on the factor loadings, industry sectors with factor loadings of 0.6 or higher were considered as primary, and the remaining industry sectors were considered as secondary sectors of that cluster (Feser & Bergman, 2000). The authors derived 28 industry clusters for manufacturing industries. However, when the data were expanded to include nonmanufacturing sectors (478 × 362 interindustry data), only 18 large cluster definitions could be derived, which were not so intuitive. Feser and Bergman (2000) mentioned that nonmanufacturing sectors such as services develop similar linkages to several types of industries, and hence, cluster definitions may include technologically dissimilar industries making it difficult to interpret intuitively.

2.2.2 *Mid-2000s*

Feser (2005) was the first study of benchmarking industry clusters based on the North American Industry Classification System (NAICS), a major departure from previous studies which had used the old SIC industry classifications to develop the industry cluster definitions. Another departure was in the methodology of identifying value chain clusters where Feser (2005) used the National IO table and Ward's hierarchical algorithm instead of the factor analysis used in previous research. The author made a case for benchmarking industry cluster definitions where clusters are derived based on interindustry purchases and sales patterns followed by geographical analysis to assess if the constituent industry sectors of a cluster are present in the region. Hence, *Benchmarking Value Chains* at the national level provided a systematic basis for economic analysis at the regional level (Feser, 2005). The premise was that certain relationships between industries are revealed in the economic space and not geographical space, and interindustry transactions (purchases and sales) in IO table at the national level are a rich source of information (Feser, 2005; Perroux, 1950). The research efforts on industry clusters during the early—and mid-2000s focused on uncovering interaction patterns in the economic and geographical spaces. It was only

[8] $X_{ij} = \frac{a_{ij}}{P_j}; X_{ji} = \frac{a_{ji}}{P_i}; Y_{ij} = \frac{a_{ij}}{S_i}; Y_{ji} = \frac{a_{ji}}{S_j}$; where X are intermediate goods purchases and Y are intermediate goods sales. There are two coefficients based on purchases and two coefficients based on sales values.

later that interactions in the social space or social networks were added to the research discourse on clusters. A chapter is dedicated to the topic of social networks and the role of networks in economic clusters.

Feser (2005) delved into explaining the strengths and weaknesses of data reduction techniques such as factor analysis versus statistical clustering algorithms, where the earlier method produced overlapping but uneven clusters and the later method produced mutually exclusive and more even clusters. However, Feser (2005) stated explicitly that "mutually exclusive industry groupings or cluster definitions are theoretically indefensible (p. 5)." Each industry has a unique value chain comprised of purchases from upstream industries (suppliers) and sales to the downstream industries (customers). Theoretically, an industry cluster contains groupings of industry sectors that share similar and linked value chains, and hence a cluster instead of a sector should be used as the unit of regional economic analysis (Feser, 2005). It should be noted that Feser (2005) built on the previous studies by Feser and Bergman (2000) and Feser and Renski (2000), which used the 1987 and 1992 National Benchmark IO tables, respectively.

The analysis commenced with a 489 × 489 interindustry transactions table obtained from the 1997 National IO accounts. The matrix was reduced to 463 × 463 after excluding service industries and government sectors. A specific set of industry sectors mostly purchasing and selling to itself and connected to very few industry sectors were termed "singletons"[9] by Feser (2005). After excluding singletons, Ward's hierarchical clustering algorithm was run on a square linkage matrix of 437 × 437 sectors. The linkage[10] was developed based on the number of sectors common in purchasing or sales sectors between two industries i and j. Unlike previous research where dollar values of flows mattered, here emphasis was on the presence or absence of sectors above a certain threshold[11] in purchasing or sales patterns between industries i and j. This eliminated the effect of outliers as evidenced in previous research. The Ward's algorithm resulted in 45 clusters or value chains of industries. Whereas the clusters were mutually exclusive due to the nature of the algorithm, Feser (2005) explored the "fuzziness" by presenting the argument[12] that an industry sector can be a member of more than one cluster based on the strength of the linkages. Feser (2005) developed another set of 15 technology-based industry clusters by using a reduced 111 × 111 sector matrix.

---

[9] NAICS 312120 (breweries) and 312140 (distilleries) were the examples of singletons.

[10] $I_{ij}^{ss} = S_i \cap S_j$; $U_{ij}^{ss} = S_i \cup S_j$; $R_{ij}^{ss} = I_{ij}^{ss} / U_{ij}^{ss}$; where measure R is a ratio of the number of supply sectors common for industries i and j to the total number of supplying sectors for i and j. A similar measure was developed for buyer sectors for i and j. Further ratios were developed between common suppliers and total buyers and vice versa to show the secondary relationships.

[11] For the supplier linkage measure, the threshold was 0.02 or 2%, and for the buyer linkage measure, it was 0.01 or 1%. For example, a sector was an important supplier if it supplied 2% or more of the total supplies to industry i or j.

[12] A sector having linkage metrics above a certain threshold to different clusters can be included as secondary member of the cluster. The results from Ward's algorithm provided clusters with primary industry sectors.

The National Benchmark Value Chain (VC) clusters by Feser (2005) were the first national template based on the NAICS system. The 45 clusters covered 64% of employment and 73% of payroll in 2004 in the United States. The research formed the basis for further national and regional cluster analyses in the United States. However, Feser (2005) cautioned that benchmarks were national templates and might not capture linkages unique to the region; however, at the same time, such information could provide guidance on targeting industry sectors which could be co-located within the regional cluster.

Scholars have been interested in the socioeconomic conditions of rural regions since the beginning of the twentieth century relying primarily on partially available data from the U.S. Decennial Census. The county geography was used substantially during and after the 1900 Decennial Census; however, it was only in 1990 and later that various census geographies were created for the entire United States, encompassing rural areas including demographic and socioeconomic data for the rural regions (Kumar & Kim, 2019; U.S. Bureau of Census, 1994). The concepts of economic competitiveness and specialization of industries that emerged during the late 1990s were applied to metropolitan regions by practitioners despite earlier efforts by Porter (2003) to use the framework for EAs for the entire United States. An advantage of benchmarked industry cluster definitions was that they could be used as a template to explore competitiveness of a region and compare the competitiveness between regions. There was a need to extend the framework for industry clusters that could benefit regions comprised of both urban and rural areas to facilitate regional development practices.

The *Unlocking Rural Competitiveness: The Role of Regional Clusters* project was commissioned to the Purdue Center for Regional Development (PCRD) in 2005. The objective was to explore a set of industry cluster definitions that were applicable to metropolitan regions including micropolitan and rural regions. The primary audiences included regions such as Economic Development Districts (EDDs), designated regions from the Economic Development Administration (EDA) serving mainly micropolitan and noncore counties, and select metropolitan counties in the United States. The research project had the following broader research questions.

What were the linkages between cluster structure, degree of rurality, and economic performances, and if cluster composition and specialization changed because of rurality and remoteness?

How are industry clusters distributed over space and what is the interface between rural and metropolitan regions?

What are the growth trajectories of counties that differ by industry clusters, rurality, and distance to metropolitan areas?

This project defined a set of 17 industry clusters at the NAICS 6-digit level. The manufacturing cluster[13] was further subdivided into six subclusters bringing the total number to 22 industry clusters. This project did not define a cluster for retail industries

[13] The manufacturing cluster comprised of industry sectors in manufacturing was termed "a supercluster" in the project.

or local services as the focus was mainly on basic industries[14] or export-oriented businesses and industry sectors. Hoyt (1954) stated that basic industries within the Economic Base Theory (EBT) were primarily classified to identify population growth in cities with the premise that employment growth would cause growth in population. Later, EBT and basic industries were used for forecasting land use requirements and local and regional economic development policies. Cluster definitions were derived based on benchmarked value chain clusters by Feser (2005); LC or co-location-based industry clusters by Porter (2003); location quotient[15]; shift-share analysis[16]; industry clusters by Nolan (2003); and a review of the previously published cluster definitions. Previous benchmarked industry clusters were used as starting points, and then, industry sectors were included or excluded based on the current co-location patterns, competitive-shift values, and the current industry cluster definitions developed by researchers and practitioners. The preliminary cluster definitions and economic metrics were applied to a case study region, the Economic Growth Region 8 of Indiana, which contained both nonmetropolitan and metropolitan counties. The feedback from regional decision-makers, local economic development offices, and planners was used to refine the industry cluster definitions and economic metrics. The project in the study region also informed how to present competitiveness analysis to the regions and develop regional economic development strategies.

The project utilized a continuous measure of the Index of Relative Rurality (IRR) by using four variables of population, population density, extent of urbanized area, and distance to the nearest metropolitan area (Waldorf, 2006). Unlike discrete measures[17] from the Economic Research Service (ERS) and the Office of Management Bureau's (OMB) metropolitan and nonmetropolitan classification, the IRR was not based on thresholds of indicator values. The index varied from

[14] In the EBT, basic industries are those industry sectors that can export goods and services outside of the region. Hoyt (1954) considered the proportion of employment in manufacturing, state and federal government, wholesale trade, transportation, and tourists as starting sectors for basic industry analysis. Later the LQ method was used to identify the basic industries.

[15] Refer to Footnote 6.

[16] Shift-share analysis could parse employment growth or decline to three influences: The effect of overall national growth or decline on a regional industry sector or cluster is known as the National Effect; the effect of the industry-level national trend on regional-level industry sector or cluster is known as the Industry Share; and regional competitiveness effect on an industry sector or a cluster is known as the Regional Share (PCRD, 2007). Despite declining trends at the national level, an industry cluster could increase its concentration or specialization at the regional level due to unique regional competitive and comparative advantages such as a skilled labor pool, the proximity to raw materials, established transportation linkages to national and global markets, and an established chain of different tiers of suppliers.

[17] ERS has developed the Rural–Urban Continuum Codes (RUCC), which divides metropolitan counties into three types and nonmetropolitan counties into six types. ERS has used population size, degree of urbanization, and adjacency to a metropolitan area as criteria to classify counties. ERS has also developed the Urban Influence Codes (UIC) that classify a county into nine categories based on population size of metro area, size of the largest town or city, and proximity to metropolitan or micropolitan counties.

0 to 1 with 0 being the most urban and 1 being the most rural counties. The IRR did not answer if a county was an "urban or rural," but what was the extent or the degree of the rurality for that county (Waldorf, 2006). Metropolitan areas contain the core and outlying area with counties located in the outskirts having rural areas. Hence, metropolitan areas are heterogenous mix of counties comprised of urban and rural parts (Waldorf, 2006). The IRR was expected to simplify the classification and hence facilitate the study between industry cluster specializations and the rurality (PCRD, 2007; Waldorf, 2006).

The study revealed that certain types of industry clusters were concentrated more toward rural areas, whereas certain industry clusters were concentrated more in urban areas. The scatter plots between IRR and the employment share of clusters revealed that business and financial services; printing and publishing; information technology and telecommunications; and biomedical/biotechnical were more urban centric (PCRD, 2007). At the same time, agribusiness, food processing and technology, mining, and forest and wood products clusters were more rural centric (PCRD, 2007). The project provided important insights into the spatial distribution of specialization of industry clusters through GIS mapping and spatial analysis. The project discovered that rural regions were not dependent on agriculture only, which was contrary to the common understanding. Regions had specializations in more than one industry cluster, and urban and/or rural parts contributed to the specializations of the industry clusters. The case study revealed that targeting a diverse group of specialized industry clusters was feasible and useful for regions. Hence, unlike the previous academic discourse on urbanization (heterogeneity) versus localization (specialization), an appropriate approach was targeting a mixed group of specialized industry clusters.

2.2.3 *Mid-2010s*

The latest effort in defining benchmarked clusters for the United States is by Delgado et al. (2015) in their publication, "*Defining Clusters of Related Industries.*" The authors classify cluster identification methods as IO linkages, co-location patterns, and knowledge clusters. The authors summarized the previous efforts highlighting the nuances in methodologies. For example, Feser and Bergman (2000) used factor analysis of IO linkage matrix, which provided an uneven group of clusters with overlapping sectors. Feser (2005) improved the method by applying hierarchical clustering on the IO linkage matrix and derived a set of 45 mutually exclusive clusters. Porter (2003) explored industry clusters based on co-location patterns or LC of employment to derive a set of 41 clusters of traded industries or sectors, which had the potential to export goods and services outside the regions, states, and the nation. Refer to Table 2.1 for details of the previous industry cluster projects in the United States.

The algorithm developed by Delgado et al. (2015) contained a similarity matrix between industry pairs. The authors extended the previous research on LC of

Table 2.1 Features of the U.S. Benchmark Industry Cluster Projects

#	Year	Author	No. of Clusters	Method	Data	Base	Journal/report	Funding source	Remarks
1	2000	Edward Feser and Edward Bergman	28	Purchase and sales coefficients of IO transactions table and factor analysis	1987 National IO	United States	National Industry Cluster Templates: A Framework for Applied Regional Cluster Analysis (Feser & Bergman, 2000)	State of North Carolina	Manufacturing industries
2	2003	Michael Porter	41	LC of employment	County Business Patterns	United States	The Economic Performance of Regions (Porter, 2003)	EDA	Traded cluster, local cluster, and resource-dependent cluster; overlapping cluster definitions
3	2005	Edward Feser	45; 18	Purchase and sales coefficients of IO transactions table and Ward's hierarchical clustering algorithm	1997 National IO	United States	Benchmarking Value Chain Clusters for Applied Regional Research (Feser, 2005)	State of North Carolina, National Science Foundation (NSF)	Value chain clusters and technology-based industry clusters
4	2007	PCRD	22	Feser (2005), Porter (2003), location quotient,	Unsuppressed QCEW (Quarterly Census of Employment and Wages)	United States	Unlocking Rural Competitiveness: The Role of Regional	EDA	Overlapping cluster definitions based on NAICS

(continued)

Table 2.1 (continued)

#	Year	Author	No. of Clusters	Method	Data	Base	Journal/report	Funding source	Remarks
				Nolan (2003), review of previously published clusters	data for Indiana; suppressed QCEW data for other states		Clusters (PCRD, 2007)		6-digit industry codes
5	2015	Mercedes Delgado, Michael Porter, and Scott Stern	51	Combined similarity matrices based on LC, IO, and occupations; hierarchical clustering; validation scores	2009 CBP data for EAs (EAs); 2002 Benchmark IO Account for United States; 2009 OES (Occupational Employment and Wage Statistics) data from BLS	United States	Defining Clusters of Related Industries (Delgado et al., 2015).	EDA	Mutually exclusive clusters based on NAICS 6-digit industry codes. Traded and local clusters

employment by Porter (2003) to include both LC of employment and establishments. Similarly, the Co-Agglomeration Index (COAI)[18] developed by Ellison and Glaeser (1997) and Ellison et al. (2010) was extended from SIC 3-digit to NAICS 6-digit by Delgado et al. (2015). The authors mention that linkages based on the national IO table reveal interindustry purchasing and selling patterns that reveal economic linkages, but do not capture relationships based on geographical characteristics. The authors computed two types of IO linkages[19] based on the maximum and average values of four unidirectional relationships between industries i and j, and hence extended the previous research by Ellison et al. (2010) and Feser (2005). The authors also developed occupation links by using occupation or staffing patterns by industry data available from the Occupational Employment Statistics, Bureau of Labor Statistics (BLS). The pairwise correlation[20] of occupation distribution between two different industries revealed if those industries were linked through skills and occupational or labor requirements (Delgado et al., 2015). Hence, the authors extended previous studies by Jun Koo, (2005a) and Glaeser and Kerr (2009).

The standardized average of four similarity matrices, LC of employment and establishments, IO_{ij} and Occ_{ij}, was used in the clustering algorithm. The authors proposed a method of clustering functions[21] and parameter choices to define groups of industry sectors into clusters by using hierarchical clustering with Ward's linkages and k-means and k-medians centroid-based clustering functions (Delgado et al., 2015). The authors developed a validation method to compare different cluster configurations including within- and between-clustering interrelationships and overlapping scores. The algorithm and process created definitions for several clusters, and in several cases, splits or mergers were made after validation. Delgado et al. (2015) developed a set of 51 mutually exclusive traded clusters for the United States. This was the last effort in developing the benchmarked cluster definitions for the United States. The authors developed a robust set of similarity matrices to explore different interrelationships between industries; however, Delgado et al. (2015) mentioned that the cluster definitions did not include patent-citation linkages (knowledge and technology) and social linkages between firms and agents such as entrepreneurs. The benchmarked cluster data and resources were distributed through dedicated websites.[22]

[18] COAI was developed for EAs. The formula is $COAI_{ij} = \sum(S_{ri} - X_r)(S_{rj} - X_r)/\left(1 - \sum X_r^2\right)$, where S_{ri} is the share of industry i employment in the region r and X_r is the mean share of employment in all industry sectors (Delgado et al., 2015).

[19] $IO_{ij} = Max\left\{input_{i\rightarrow j}, input_{i\leftarrow j}, output_{i\rightarrow j}, output_{i\leftarrow j}\right\}$(Delgado et al., 2015).

[20] $Occ_{ij} = Correlation\left(Occupation_i, Occupation_j\right)$ (Delgado et al., 2015).

[21] $C = F\left(M_{ij}, \beta\right)$; Where *Mij* is combined similarity matrix and β is the parameter choices. Note that the clustering algorithm requires a minimum number of clusters as inputs.

[22] https://www.isc.hbs.edu/about-michael-porter/affiliated-organizations-institutions/Pages/us-cluster-mapping-project.aspx;; https://clustermapping.us/.

2.2.4 Knowledge-based Industry Clusters

There has been significant research and discussions on the mechanisms for knowledge spillovers; however, limited works have occurred in identifying the interrelatedness between knowledge and industries. This is the reason for the lack of knowledge-based industry clusters in the United States, irrespective of the pre- and post-2010 research on clusters explained previously. Feldman and Audretsch (1999) identified six industry clusters based on commonalities of R&D[23] activities in specific academic disciplines. Industry sectors within the cluster were engaged in research, innovation, and product development from the same academic disciplines. While the industries within the cluster or group[24] shared the same knowledge and innovation research base, the geographic distribution and product development could be disparate (Feldman & Audretsch, 1999). This research extended the debate between diversification and specialization by finding evidence that variety in production promoted innovation and in turn triggered economic growth in the regions. The research by Feldman and Audretsch (1999) supported Jacobs' (1969) findings that knowledge spillovers among diverse industries promoted regional economic growth in contrast to the Marshall–Arrow–Romer (MAR)[25] hypothesis on specialization of industries and spillovers within the firms causing economic growth in the regions. At the heart of this debate lie the two contrasting viewpoints. The first was on local specialization and concentration and knowledge spillover within the same group of industries as elucidated by the MAR hypothesis. The other viewpoint was that urbanization encouraged industrial variety and competitions causing knowledge spillovers between diverse industries as elucidated by Glaeser et al. (1992) and Jacobs (1969). Compared to the product innovation pursued by Feldman and Audretsch (1999); J. Koo (2005) utilized cited patents in manufacturing industries to derive knowledge-based industry clusters. However, post-2005, new research on knowledge-based industry clusters has been limited.

2.2.5 Integrated Industry Clusters

It is evident that industry clusters have been explored by different researchers through different lenses, especially the methods to define the clusters. Vom Hofe

[23] Research and Development.

[24] The six groups were identified by using the Yale Survey of R&D Managers and the Small Business Administration's Innovation Data Base.

[25] Marshall, Arrow, and Romer (MAR) published their seminal works in 1890, 1962, and 1986, respectively. Together it is known as the MAR Model for specialization-based regional growth. According to MAR, regional growth happens because of industrial growth, where the specialization or concentration of similar industries causes knowledge spillovers among firms within the same industry sector (Beaudry & Schiffauerova, 2009).

and Chen (2006) found that the common understanding that industry clusters included a group of interrelated industry sectors, institutions, labor force, suppliers, and buyers has been consistent through the decades; however, scholars had employed different methodologies including IO, LQ, shift-share, and other methods. This resulted in different industry cluster definitions over the decades because of the lack of "rigorous microeconomic foundations" to identify industry clusters (Vom Hofe & Chen, 2006). The lack of a microeconomic foundation might have led to different industry cluster definitions; however, it also provided an opportunity to explore various methodologies including quantitative and qualitative methods. Note that the benchmarked clusters reviewed in this section employed quantitative methods. However, a recent study on the most commonly used methods to identify industry clusters emphasized the role of qualitative analysis or interviews and expert focus groups to understand and define industry clusters (Komorowski, 2020). Academicians and practitioners are discovering that the industry cluster framework has applications beyond the traditional economic development field.

In the past, industry cluster strategies and initiatives had focused solely on increasing competitiveness and regional economic growth, and in so doing ignored the critical aspects of the distribution of the economic growth across the society. However, a recent effort by Wilkinson et al. (2024) initiated addressing this gap by exploring the development of integrated clusters. The authors used interviews of experts and case studies to analyze how industry cluster initiatives are addressing the issue of the distribution of resources in the United States. The authors share some important lessons to develop and incubate the industry clusters, which include "starting with the committed leadership; planning and budgeting for engagement efforts; and building trust and business support systems that are time-consuming but critical for success" (Wilkinson et al., 2024).

2.3 Data Limitations

It is evident that scholars have used a variety of public data sources to define and analyze industry clusters in the United States. However, there have been challenges because of the lack of granularity and suppression in the publicly available data. The most commonly used data sources were the national IO table of industry flows from BEA; jobs and establishments data from CBP, U.S. Census Bureau; jobs and establishments data from the QCEW available from the BLS; and OES from the BLS. Refer to Table 2.1 for data sources used in various industry clusters benchmarking projects in the United States.

Over the decades, these data sources changed substantially in terms of coverage and types of variables. This makes the temporal analysis substantially challenging. For example, the benchmark IO tables from BEA are published every 5 years during the economic census period. The 2017 benchmark IO table shows intermediate industry transactions for a group of 402 industry sectors. At the same time,

NAICS classified 1,057 industry sectors at the 6-digit level in 2017. There is a precision and scale mismatch between vital information on industry-to-industry flows and industry sector employment data. The annual IO table for 2022 provides intermediate industry transactions for only 72 industry sectors. Compared to 1,012 NAICS 6-digit industry sectors in 2022, the IO table from BEA is only marginally helpful in deciphering detailed industry-to-industry flows. The lack of granularity and the suppression in public data remain a challenge even after decades of public data availability.

The NAICS codes for industries decreased in numbers at the most granular 6-digit level for every economic census period. For example, there were 1,179 NAICS 6-digit codes during the 2002 Economic Census; however, the NAICS 6-digit codes decreased to 1,012 in the 2022 Economic Census. For CBP 2021 county-level data, 41% of manufacturing sector data were noted with high noise[26] at the NAICS 6-digit level. For the NAICS 2-digit level, 19% of data were noted with the high noise. The noise was added to the published numbers in the CBP data instead of suppression. For QCEW, 10% of data were suppressed in 2022 for manufacturing sectors at the NAICS 2-digit level. The suppression increased to 85% for counties at the NAICS 6-digit level. The BEA provides economic metrics for industry sectors at only NAICS 2-digit levels. For U.S. manufacturing, 11% of BEA data were suppressed for NAICS 2-digits at the county level.[27] The NAICS 2-digits provide only a broad overview of the industry sectors, and the 2-digit codes are not useful for developing industry cluster definitions. However, the NAICS 2-digit data can provide important insights into the employment distribution in major industry sectors. Research on industry clusters requires detailed establishment, employment, and earnings data for industries, and the high suppression levels in public datasets pose significant challenges.

2.4 Conclusion and Paths Forward

There have been five specific initiatives to develop benchmarked industry cluster definitions in the United States during the years 2000, 2003, 2005, 2007, and 2015, respectively. These research initiatives utilized a variety of data sources from BEA, BLS, and the Census Bureau of the United States to develop industry cluster definitions that could be applied to different U.S. regions. As elucidated by the term "benchmark," the cluster definitions provided a template and framework for regional economic competitiveness analysis comparing peer, competitor, or aspirant regions. Over the decades, the data sources have become comprehensive;

[26] The high noise means that the original data have been changed by 5% or more to protect the confidentiality. https://www.census.gov/programs-surveys/cbp/technical-documentation/methodology.html#par_textimage_245304869.

[27] As of the preparation of this chapter, BEA has discontinued county-level industry employment data from November 2024. The last data are available for the year 2023.

however, the challenges of data suppression and time lag remain. Previous research efforts have used a mix of qualitative and quantitative methodologies including a review of existing definitions of industry clusters, economic IO analysis, and various correlational measures. The scholars stated that production and spillovers of innovation such as patent-citations linkages data were sparse and hence could not be used to inform cluster definitions. Similarly, suppression of economic data at the granular level of NAICS codes for substate geographies creates information gaps despite un-suppression methods utilized by researchers and proprietary data sources.

Recent efforts by scholars extend the field further by exploring the heterogeneity in agglomeration and uncovering reasons for co-location in industries. For example, Diodato et al. (2018) found that unlike previous decades, the primary reason for industries to co-locate at present is because of similar skills and opportunities for skill-sharing between industries. Similarly, Kalathil et al. (2025) found that the types of agglomeration and their intensities can vary by regions. The horizontal agglomeration or co-location of similar types of firms can happen in manufacturing industries, but vertical agglomeration or co-location of diverse types of firms can be observed in more R&D and STEM[28] occupation-intensive sectors such as specialized services that support manufacturing industries (Kalathil et al., 2025). Delgado and Mills (2020) postulate that innovation happens not only in manufacturing but also in the "supply side" comprised of both goods and services. Scholars are exploring the concepts of product space or relatedness between products and sophistication of products, and their roles in transitioning from developing to developed economies (Hidalgo et al., 2007). Because of the product relatedness, regions can identify "implied or potential comparative advantages" even in production areas not present in the regions (Hausmann et al., 2022). These research efforts emphasize the emerging topics and themes for the future research directions related to industry clusters and competitiveness.

References

Arthur, B. W. (1990). Positive feedback in the economy. *Scientific American, 262*(2), 92–99.

Beaudry, C., & Schiffauerova, A. (2009). Who's right, Marshall or Jacobs? The localization versus urbanization debate. *Research Policy, 38*, 318–337.

Bergman, E., & Feser, E. (1999). *Industrial and regional clusters: Concepts and comparative advantages*. Reprint Edited by S. Loveridge & R. Jackson WVU Research Repository 2020.

Bruilhart, M. (2009). Is the new economic geography passe? VOX[EU]. https://cepr.org/voxeu/columns/new-economic-geography-passe#fn1. Accessed on September 15, 2024.

Cortright, J. (2006). *Making sense of clusters: Regional competitiveness and economic development*. The Brookings Institution.

Czamanski, S., & Augusto de Q. A. L. (1979). Identification of industrial clusters and complexes. *Urban Studies, 16*, 61–80.

[28] Science Technology Engineering and Mathematics.

Delgado, M., & Mills, K. G. (2020). The supply chain economy: A new industry categorization for understanding innovation in services. *Research Policy*, *49*, 104039.

Delgado, M., Porter, M., & Stern, S. (2015). Defining clusters of related industries. *Journal of Economic Geography*, *16*(1), 1–38.

Diodato, D., Nefke, F., & O'Clery, N. (2018). Why do industries coagglomerate? How Marshallian externalities differ by industry and have evolved over time. *Journal of Urban Economics*, *106*, 1–26.

Ellison, G., & Glaeser, E. L. (1997). Geographic concentration in U.S. manufacturing industries: A dartboard approach. *Journal of Political Economy*, *105*(5), 899–927.

Ellison, G., Glaeser, E. L., & Kerr, W. (2010). What causes industry agglomeration? Evidence from conglomeration patterns. *American Economic Review*, *100*, 1195–1213.

Feldman, M., & Audretsch, D. (1999). Innovation in cities: Science-based diversity, specialization and localized competition. *European Economic Review*, *43*, 409–429.

Feser, E. (2005). Benchmarking value chain clusters for applied regional research. In *Regional Economics Applications Laboratory*. University of Illinois Urbana Champaign (UIUC).

Feser, E., & Bergman, E. (2000). National industry cluster templates: A framework for applied regional cluster analysis. *Regional Studies*, *34*(1), 1–19.

Feser, E., & Renski, H. (2000). High-tech clusters in North Carolina. North Carolina Board of Science and Technology. https://www.commerce.nc.gov/high-tech-clusters-north-carolina-2000-0/open#:~:text=The%20core%20U.S.%20technology%20clusters,and%20pharmaceuticals%20and%20medical%20technologies. Accessed on May 6, 2024.

Glaeser, E., Kallal, H. D., Scheinkman, J. A., & Shleifer, A. (1992). Growth in cities. *Journal of Political Economy*, *100*(6), 1126–1152.

Glaeser, E. L., & Kerr, W. R. (2009). Local industrial conditions and entrepreneurship: How much of the spatial distribution can we explain? *Journal of Economics and Management Strategy*, *18*(3), 623–663.

Hausmann, R., Stock, D. P., & Yildirim, M. A. (2022). Implied comparative advantage. *Research Policy*, *51*, 104143.

Hidalgo, C. A., Klinger, B., Barabasi, A. L., & Hausmann, R. (2007). The product space conditions the development of nations. *Science*, *317*, 482–487.

Hoyt, H. (1954). Homer Hoyt on development of economic base concept. *Land Economics*, *30*(2), 182–186.

Jacobs, J. (1969). *The economy of cities*. Random House.

Johnson, K. P., & Kort, J. R. (2004). 2004 Redefinition of the BEA economic areas. https://apps.bea.gov/scb/pdf/2004/11November/1104Econ-areas.pdf?_gl=1*1tam6wu*_ga*MTkxNTgxODQzNC4xNzI2NTkxNzA4*_ga_J4698JNNFT*MTcyNjU5MTcwOC4xLjEuMTcyNjU5MTcxOS40OS4wLjA. Accessed on September 17, 2024.

Kadokawa, K. (2011). Applicability of Marshall's Agglomeration Theory to industrial clustering in the Japanese manufacturing sector: An exploratory factor analysis approach. *The Journal of Regional Analysis and Policy*, *41*(2), 83–100.

Kalathil, N., Lanahan, L., Feldman, M., & H Fuchs, E. R. (2025). Varieties of agglomeration: Disentangling horizontal and vertical agglomeration within the manufacturing sector in the United States. *Research Policy*, *54*, 105272.

Komorowski, M. (2020). Identifying industry clusters: A critical analysis of the most commonly used methods. *Regional Studies, Regional Science*, *7*(1), 92–100.

Koo, J. (2005). Knowledge-based industry clusters: Evidenced by geographical patterns of patents in manufacturing. *Urban Studies*, *42*(9), 1487–1505.

Koo, J. (2005a). How to analyze the regional economy with occupation data. *Economic Development Quarterly*, *19*(4), 356–372.

Krugman, P. (1991). Increasing returns and economic geography. *Journal of Political Economy*, *99*(3), 483–499.

Kumar, I., & Kim, Y. J. (2019). *Spatial data documentation: Intergenerational transfer of poverty project 2015–2017*. Purdue Center for Regional Development and Department of Agricultural Economics, Purdue University.
Kumar, I., Zhalnin, A., Kim, A., & Beaulieu, L. (2017). Transportation and logistics cluster competitive advantages in the U.S. regions: A cross-sectional and spatio-temporal Analysis. *Research in Transportation Economics*, *61*, 25–36.
Marshall, A. (1890). Principles of economics. Macmillan and Co. 8th ed. 1920: London. https://oll.libertyfund.org/titles/marshall-principles-of-economics-8th-ed. Accessed on Apr 15, 2024.
Myrdal, G. (1957). *Economic theory and under-developed regions*. G. Duckworth.
Nijkamp, P., Kourtit, K., Krugman, P., & Moreno, C. (2024). Old wisdom and the new economic geography: Managing uncertainty in twenty-first century regional and urban development. *Regional Science Policy and Practice*, *16*, 100124.
Nolan, C. E. (2003). Hamilton county's comparative and competitive advantages: Business and industry clusters *Community COMPASS Special Report*Vols. 3–6 Hamilton County Regional Planning Commission.
O'hUallachain, B. (1984). The identification of industrial complexes. *Annals of the Association of American Geographers*, *74*(3), 420–436.
Perroux, F. (1950). Economic space: Theory and applications. *The Quarterly Journal of Economics*, *64*(1), 89–104.
Porter, M. (1990). The competitive advantage of nations. *Harvard Business Review*. https://hbr.org/1990/03/the-competitive-advantage-of-nations. Accessed on May 25, 2024.
Porter, M. (1998). Clusters and the new economics of competition. *Harvard Business Review*. https://biblioteca.fundacionicbc.edu.ar/images/d/de/Clusters_1.pdf. Accessed on May 26, 2024.
Porter, M. (2003). The economic performance of regions. *Regional Studies*, *37*(6–7), 549–578.
Purdue Center for Regional Development (PCRD). (2007). Unlocking rural competitiveness: The role of regional clusters. Technical Project Report available at. https://pcrd.purdue.edu/wp-content/uploads/2021/10/unlocking_rural_competitiveness_full_report.pdf. Accessed on June 8, 2024.
Sheppard, E. (2017). Economic theory and underdeveloped regions. *Regional Studies*, *51*(6), 972–973.
U.S. Bureau of the Census. (1994). *Geographic areas reference manual. U.S.* Department of Commerce.
Vom Hofe, R., & Chen, K. (2006). Whether or not industrial clusters: Conclusions or confusions? *The Industrial Geographer*, *4*(1), 2–28.
Waldorf, B. (2006). A continuous multi-dimensional measure of rurality: Moving beyond threshold measures. Paper presented at Annual Meeting of the Association of Agricultural Economics, July 2006, Long Beach, California.
Wilkinson, J., Suchanic, B., & McCarty, M. Y. (2024). Developing inclusive clusters. Insight Report. RTI International.

Chapter 3
Economic Geography of Knowledge and Innovation: National and International Contexts

Cheyanne Geideman, Hyewon Shin, and Indraneel Kumar

Abstract This chapter explores knowledge and innovation through the lens of economic geography, focusing on the U.S. and international case studies. The chapter presents the nuances, in particular, the channels of learning, transfer, and management of knowledge. It delves into terms such as epistemic community and tacit knowledge. The dynamic flow from knowledge sharing into entrepreneurship and innovation in the industry cluster setting is also discussed. The chapter presents several case studies of industry clusters, including international examples of manufacturing and high-technology clusters, as well as cultural districts. The chapter concludes by exploring the roles of industry clusters in developmental pathways such as modernism and economic and human development.

Keywords Innovation · Epistemic community · Tacit knowledge · Knowledge transfer · Human development

There is substantial research on knowledge and innovation spillovers and diffusion processes in economics, geography, and planning as researchers have tried to understand mechanisms of economic growth. Knowledge production, knowledge transfer and diffusion, innovation production and spillovers, national and regional innovation systems, and innovative milieux are a few terms coined by researchers to describe the processes in the knowledge

C. Geideman
Purdue Extension, Purdue University, West Lafayette, IN, USA
e-mail: cgeidema@purdue.edu

H. Shin · I. Kumar (✉)
Purdue Center for Regional Development, Purdue University, West Lafayette, IN, USA
e-mail: shin457@purdue.edu
e-mail: ikumar@purdue.edu

I. Kumar, R. Gallardo (eds.), *Economic Competitiveness*, SpringerBriefs in Regional Science,
https://doi.org/10.1007/978-3-032-20359-5_3

and innovation space. Feldman (2000) has described the vast literature on knowledge and innovation in two categories—(1) innovation as an output in the production function using geography as the unit of analysis and other descriptors; and (2) innovation as one of the descriptors to explain differences in economic growth and productivity between regions. Innovation is entered as a dependent variable in the first category, and it is an independent variable in the second category of such studies. The geographical units are "regions" and not "local" or "national" that are intrinsic to both the categories of research to provide the spatial contexts (Feldman, 2000).

Schumpeter is credited with developing the concept and role of innovation in economic development identifying five types of innovations that include new products, new materials, new production processes, new markets, and new organizational forms (Ziemnowicz, 2013). Innovation, entrepreneurship, and "Creative Destruction" were central to Schumpeterian thinking of mechanisms for economic development (Ziemnowicz, 2013). Many scholars have also explored the role of agglomeration in enabling knowledge creation, diffusion, and innovation. Within agglomeration, especially the role of urbanization and the diversification of industries, institutions, employers, labor force, and residents have been explored in facilitating innovations and spillovers such as patents, citations, trademarks, technologies, and ideas (Feldman, 2000; Jacobs, 1969; Jaffe et al., 1993).

The geography of production has, in part, explained the geography of innovation as specialization and proximity of firms have facilitated the knowledge spillovers. Yet researchers have also found that investments in the industry Research and Development (R&D), university research, and concentration of skilled workers were significant in explaining the innovation outputs (Audretsch & Feldman, 1996). Hence, the geographies of production, knowledge, and innovation have important spatial aspects requiring further research. In addition to agglomeration and specialization of factors of production, research has also revealed "culture" as an important determinant for innovation as revealed by Saxenian's insightful research on the technological success of Silicon Valley and the role of open social networks (Saxenian, 1996).

The knowledge development process is a continuum. An accepted general pathway is "information—knowledge—wisdom." Whereas the cost of transferring information over large distances has declined because of the progress in internet and data storage technologies, there are limitations on how knowledge can be transferred, especially through the mechanisms of spillovers and incentives of economic gains. This chapter delves into the spatial and aspatial aspects of knowledge and innovation systems from the lens of agglomeration and regional development. It also includes international cases of industry clusters as different developmental pathways.

3.1 Knowledge and Collective Learning

The conversion of information to knowledge is a collective learning process. However, knowledge development and knowledge management are distinct processes. Effective knowledge management can be achieved through developing operational routines, standards, norms, and social interactions and communications. The ability to manage this chain of processes determines the competency of the organizations. Knowledge management is directly connected to firms' competitiveness. In the industry cluster setting, strategic alliances, competition, and cooperation are actively pursued through knowledge sharing and resource integration activities. Joint efforts in R&D and innovation in the industry clusters contribute to strengthening firms' international competitiveness (Lai et al., 2014). The knowledge transmission and collective learning are fostered by cultural, institutional, and geographical proximity. Networks and dependencies might have significant effects on the competitive performance of organizations (Keeble & Wilkinson, 1999). Here, the authors have defined two types of knowledge, which include codifiable and tacit knowledge. The codifiable knowledge is readily transferrable, whereas the tacit knowledge is embedded within the context; therefore, it is not readily transferrable (Keeble & Wilkinson, 1999).

3.2 Knowledge Transfer and Epistemic Community

Lissoni (2001) discussed knowledge codification and innovation in clusters of small- and medium-sized enterprises (SMEs) in Italy. The case study of the top three sectors in Italy's Brescia's machinery industries showed that industry clusters are better at facilitating tacit knowledge production, and the knowledge circulates within the epistemic communities of professionals and workers sharing similar occupations, training, knowledge, skills, and abilities. The epistemic communities are formed by professionals in common enterprises who share the common professional language and vocational frameworks, and these communities extend beyond individual organizations (Hakanson, 2005; Loasby, 1998). Lissoni (2001) also discussed localized labor mobility and knowledge socialization as the main contributors to knowledge transfers, which included firms and establishments, workers, suppliers, and even customers.

Breschi and Lissoni (2001) defined localized knowledge spillovers (LKSs) as a public good and a positive externality. It is tacit in nature and difficult to codify or transfer. Hence, LKS allows companies operating in spatial proximity to access key knowledge sources and innovations faster. Technical knowledge can be highly specific and dynamic, which can be acquired through practical experiences, but tacit exchange is still possible. The LKS econometrics have used the knowledge production function, emphasizing the impact of external R&D on a private firm's innovation capabilities. R&D and patents are used as core variables to measure an individual firm's innovation capabilities.

Industry clusters are the concentration of interlinked industries, and firms within the cluster can access tacit knowledge which can provide competitive advantages to those firms. The professionals in the cluster belong to the same or related epistemic communities (Hakanson, 2005; Loasby, 1998). These epistemic communities extend beyond individual organizations. For knowledge-based industries, socialization and vocational trainings lead to professional communities and networks with common codes, technical language, and understanding. In this epistemic community, both codified and tacit knowledge move easily. Some epistemic communities are geographically concentrated like communities clustering around Silicon Valley, but long-distance communication and collaboration among firms allow development of epistemic communities across geographical boundaries (Hakanson, 2005).

3.3 Knowledge Management to Innovation

3.3.1 Systemic Support in Knowledge Management

Geographical or spatial proximity allows knowledge to circulate among local actors, and informal contacts play key roles in transferring knowledge and information. Firms relocated into the industry cluster benefit from these positive externalities. For example, Morrison (2008) described the role of leader firms in furniture industries in southern Italy in shaping the district's learning processes. Leading firms in the industrial districts can build stronger capacity and access a larger set of external information and knowledge sources. They play a leading role in shaping industrial districts and are at the core of multilevel knowledge networks. For complex knowledge and transfer mechanisms, leader firms can develop strategies in implementing knowledge translation and codification function (Morrison, 2008). The leading firms play the role of knowledge gatekeepers who would identify external sources, absorb them, and then translate and disseminate external knowledge through local-level learning activities (Allen, 1977; Morrison, 2008). The concept of knowledge gatekeeper provides useful insights into the processes of learning and knowledge diffusion. Gatekeepers are a small community of individuals who are the core nodes of the information network and have informal linkages with external actors. Gatekeepers will search, transcode, and share knowledge for the actors in the organization (Allen, 1977; Morrison, 2008).

Local business organizations and trade associations play important roles in organizing events such as trade shows, industry conferences, and social activities. These events give valuable opportunities for participants to connect, exchange contacts, and share technical and market information. Trade associations play a critical role in providing technical, financial, marketing, training, and other support services and representing employers in dealing with the government and organized labor (Keeble & Wilkinson, 1999).

Innovation should be understood as a cycle involving interactions between tacit and articulated knowledge (Keeble & Wilkinson, 1999; Lawson & Lorenz, 1999). The ability to share and use varied knowledge leads to the success of high-technology regions. For example, interactions between technology user and producer, multidisciplinary culture of a local university, and links between large and small firms are channels of knowledge flows.

3.3.2 Innovation Milieux and Entrepreneurial Activities

Innovation processes have been discussed by many scholars in relation to knowledge and competence. Innovative Milieux is the term adopted by European researchers to describe local clustering of highly innovative producers of high-technology products and services. To achieve continued success in innovative milieux, learning from external knowledge is essential (Keeble & Wilkinson, 1999). Industrial districts generate high levels of trust and encourage informal and tacit knowledge transfer. This leads to an industrial atmosphere, external economies, and savings in transaction costs. Synergies and innovative capacity are created by cooperative relations facilitating knowledge transfer. In this process, industrial districts become innovative milieux (Capello, 1999; Keeble & Wilkinson, 1999).

Lai et al. (2014) discussed the relationship between knowledge management of industry cluster and innovation performance. Knowledge management is defined as an all-encompassing process which spans from knowledge creation, acquisition to dissemination, and storage. Innovation performance is measured by market performance and product performance. Empirical analysis based on survey questionnaires collected from the Taiwanese industry clusters including science parks, export processing zones, and industrial zones supported the main hypotheses that firms can utilize resources more effectively within the industry cluster environment and achieve higher competitiveness. Industry clusters allow firms to manage more effective knowledge management and raise the level of innovation performance.

Hakanson (2005) outlined a model of cluster dynamics and key factors leading to the following outcome: Growth in industry clusters is derived from flows of the various factors such as growth of existing firms, high rate of new firm formation, positive environment for entrepreneurship, competitive technological advancement and innovation opportunities, and resource inflows through globalization (Hakanson, 2005). Cluster setting provides easy access and varied opportunities to both entrepreneurs and job seekers, and the active formation of new firms and their accomplishments plays an important role in continuation and growth of the cluster (Hakanson, 2005).

3.4 Industry Cluster Case Studies

3.4.1 Manufacturing

Schmitz and Musyck (1994) discussed the role of formal institutions in four European industrial districts including the Third Italy, Baden-Wurttemberg in Southern Germany, West Jutland in Denmark, and South-West Flanders in Belgium. Institutions can help in new technology development, new market identification, skilled labor training, and raising capital. In these European industry district examples, local credit institutions, regional systems, and regional governmental support played a critical role in fostering small- and medium-sized firms in the region. Vocational and technical training programs for both workers and entrepreneurs were widely used and fostered in these regions. Provision of local-level training and apprenticeship, training programs for entrepreneurs, and courses on technical and managerial issues were also provided. A dual system of vocational training and education was offered through vocational training colleges in the region. The Chamber of Commerce and Industry, professional associations, and training and technology centers played a significant role in the dual educational and training system. Regional governments played an important role in pursuing active innovation efforts. In addition, regional and local associations contributed to develop strategic policies to support industrial districts with small- and medium-sized firms (Schmitz & Musyck, 1994).

3.4.2 High-Technology

Gray et al. (1996) called Seattle a hub-and-spoke industrial district where a region hosts one or more industries with one or a few dominant firms or nonprofit institutions. The case study examined Seattle's three major high-technology industries including aerospace, software, and biotechnology. Boeing was the single most important hub for aerospace activities. The software hub was formed due to Boeing's internal needs. The biotechnology hub was formed independently. The three successful industry hubs generated agglomeration economies, enriched infrastructure, and strengthened resistance to disruptions in the region. Federal procurement, projects, and subsidies were critical in the development of both aerospace and software hubs. The role of the University of Washington and Fred Hutchinson Cancer Research Center was significant in the development of the biotechnology hub in the areas of R&D and entrepreneurial opportunities.

3.4.3 *Culture*

Santagata (2002) defined culture as the capital asset accumulated by community reflecting tangible and intangible identity. Both material and nonmaterial culture-based goods are created through human creativity and intellectual activities during this distinctive process. In Europe, cultural markets provided major employment in the region. Industrial cultural districts initially started with many SMEs such as the Third Italy. Within industrial cultural districts, enterprises were benefiting from the low cost of use of the market due to positive externalities, tacit knowledge, high rate of innovation, and easy networking. Two types of positive externalities from the creation of industrial cultural district were identified by Santagata (2002): (1) Atelier effect focusing on training local cultural professions and creating entrepreneurial opportunities, and (2) new product creation and differentiation through the new product creation process.

Italy's museum cultural district is composed of a network of museums. The museum district impacts include increased demand for hotel and tourism services, boosting international reputation, and positive externalities including network, consumption, time, and economy of scale. Metropolitan cultural districts are concentrated with buildings such as performing arts, museums, and organizations producing cultural events, goods, and services. Many metropolitan cities are hosts to the metropolitan cultural districts. Art markets, performing arts, museums, cultural heritage sites, and design-based goods can be chains of value creation. Culture and cultural districts hold economic significance and help the regions thrive. It is to be noted that such districts represent a clustering of performing arts services, tourism-related activities, and creative occupations.

3.5 The International Perspective on Industry Clusters

Whereas the industry cluster strategy lends itself to a local or regional perspective, they do not function in isolation. Globalization has shifted traditional business in many ways, including bringing in competition from abroad. Understanding how industry clusters operate in a global context provides further insights into the potentials of this strategy. In addition, when looking at the international literature, case studies of industry clusters in a variety of contexts become available. Through examining the common themes from the literature, one can better understand industry clusters and their applications.

3.5.1 Recurring Characteristics from International Case Studies

The literature highlights a wide range of case studies of industry clusters across the globe. Previously, we discussed the history and definition of industry clusters. In this section, we are going to review some of the common characteristics seen in the international literature on industry clusters. The Sinos Valley industry cluster case study brought forward several characteristics that are thematic across case studies (Schmitz, 1995). These include the following: (1) importance of place and proximity, (2) competitiveness within the cluster, (3) cooperation and collective action, and (4) culture within the cluster. The following sections will dive deeper into each of these themes, bringing in examples from the literature.

3.5.1.1 The Importance of Place and Proximity

Place and proximity have been recurring discussion points throughout the literature. As stated in chapter two, geographic concentration is a key feature of industry clusters. But where the cluster is and the proximity of enterprises both have effects that are recurring topics of discussion in the literature. In Asheim and Isaksen (2002), three industry clusters in Norway are examined. These examples highlight how enterprises within an industry cluster leverage regional resources to be competitive at a global level. In addition, the Sinos Valley example (Schmitz, 1995) demonstrates how the proximity of firms leads to innovations resulting in new SMEs focused on specialized niches. In addition, with businesses being clustered together in close proximity, it allows them to cooperate on shared issues, so everyone benefits. The cooperation and collective action present in industry clusters is further explored in the next section.

3.5.1.2 Cooperation and Collective Action

Despite the competition among enterprises, cooperation for the common good is a theme across industry clusters. As mentioned previously, the Sinos Valley's shoemaking industry cluster is a prime example of how collective action is not only a characteristic of industry clusters, but can also strengthen the cluster (Schmitz, 1995). To become globally competitive, the enterprises in Sinos Valley worked together to host industry events that brought foreign buyers to them. This exposure facilitated interest and business deals between Sinos Valley and the United States. Other examples of cooperation within industry clusters include sharing resources to cultivate training opportunities to skill up the workforce. This is further underscored by the findings of Asheim (1996) that interfirm collaboration is essential to facilitating learning networks.

3.5.1.3 Competitiveness within the Cluster

When operating in a global context, competition is abundant. However, enterprises often focus on competition within their industry cluster. Buyers are looking to source products at the lowest cost possible, but when presented with competing bids from outside Sinos Valley, enterprises did not react. But once presented with a competitor's pricing from within the Sinos Valley, firms were quick to try and undercut one another.

3.5.1.4 Culture within the Cluster

A unique culture develops within industry clusters. In fact, the industry becomes part of the identity of those involved. This is partly due to how small the world is within the cluster, as one can frequently run into the same people. For this reason, relationships often are not just for economic gains. A level of trust is built that helps facilitate the collaboration mentioned previously.

3.5.2 Industry Clusters as a Road to Development

When looking at industry clusters in an international context, a key discussion point is their role in development. The process of development is a well-studied topic with differing opinions and is no different when it comes to industry clusters. Industry clusters have been exemplified as a "high road" to development, but also criticized. In this section, we will explore arguments on both sides by taking a step back and defining what we mean by development. These definitions will then be discussed alongside the arguments for and against industry clusters to highlight the breadth and depth of the ongoing discussion.

In her book *Theories and Practices of Development*, Katie Willis presents three schools of thought on how development is defined: economic, modernity, and human (Willis, 2011, Ch. 1). Development as an economic process focuses on expanding economic activities, both buying and selling among individuals and enterprises. This is especially popular in capitalist societies as many assume "that with greater wealth come other benefits such as improved health, education, and quality of life" (Willis, 2011, p. 5). Interpreting development as becoming modern is less of an exact science, as what is modern or current is a goalpost constantly on the move. It is also subjective, changing based on cultural, economic, or political contexts. Finally, the human development perspective focuses on improving the quality of life for people. From health and well-being to happiness and freedoms, this can include a range of topics. Regardless of what definition one can use, development is multifaceted, requiring examination of multiple factors. The following sections will examine the industry cluster strategy from these different perspectives.

3.5.2.1 Industry Clusters as a Road to Economic Development

With the many dimensions of development in mind, we can begin to examine the discussion around industry clusters as a tool for development. In the case study of Torreon's Blue Jeans industry in Mexico as well as the Sinos Valley's Shoemaking industry in Brazil, the researchers question the economic development for individuals and the workforce. A key piece of this discussion is the wages for workers within the cluster. While wages may be better within the industry cluster than workers could otherwise expect, the low wages are still criticized. As buyers push to lower the bottom line, the cuts ultimately come from workers' wages. The insufficient wages still leave many workers trapped, and this is expected to continue as the current model depends on lowering the costs through lowering the wages. Without the lower costs, North American buyers could source these products closer to home or find someplace else to provide the cheap labor. Many workers dream of climbing the ladder within the cluster by starting their own businesses, but the Sinos Valley example demonstrates how this has become harder as time has progressed. And in the case of Torreon's blue jean industry, U.S. contractors are documented as repeatedly returning to the same enterprises, making it hard for new ones to break in (Bair and Gereffi, 2001). Due to the low wages and limited upward mobility for workers, the economic development achieved from the industry cluster model becomes questionable for the individual or workforce in the context of the developing economies.

However, there have been several beneficial economic outcomes within the clusters. In the case of the Sinos Valley, the researchers examined the industry cluster over time which revealed the growth of several enterprises. In addition, many enterprises have been started over the decades in this cluster with varying lifespans. The geographic proximity and the expertise within the workforce have helped facilitate these start-ups and growth, leading to collaboration within the cluster as enterprises outsource aspects of production to specialty firms. For both Sinos Valley and Torreon, the clusters saw significant growth when foreign buyers started purchasing from within the cluster. In addition, while wages may be low, they are comparably higher than they would otherwise be outside of the cluster. Ultimately, there is significant economic development facilitated through the industry cluster model as it provides many opportunities for currency to exchange hands within the industry, as well as bringing in funds and resources from outside the country.

3.5.2.2 Industry Clusters as a Road to Modernity

In terms of industry clusters as a tool for modernity, there are mixed arguments as well. Modernity goes hand in hand with innovation and upgrading. Upgrading has been defined as "the capacity of a firm to innovate to increase the value added of its products and processes" (Giuliani et al., 2005). Much research has focused on how and why firms innovate within clusters, because upgrading and innovation impact a cluster's ability to be globally competitive (Asheim, 1996). And many characteristics of industry clusters aid in innovation. In the examples in Norway (Asheim & Isaksen, 2002), the enterprises take advantage of local and regional education resources for upgrading. Similarly, in the Sinos Valley, the opportunities for collaboration between enterprises have led to the development of niche expertise for SMEs. By integrating their work into the production process, large enterprises have added additional value to their products (Schmitz, 1995). In the modern age, this innovation extends to technology. To keep up with one another, firms adopt new technologies and make improvements, leading to technical advances coming from within industry clusters.

However, the limitations foreign buyers impose can limit innovation. This is seen in the Torreon industry cluster, as U.S. buyers limit in what ways the enterprises can upgrade by insisting certain parts of the process be done in the United States versus in Torreon, Mexico. Further, a handful of the enterprises have a monopoly on the contracts from the United States and are gatekeepers for smaller enterprises. Without the prospect of more business, enterprises do not have the incentive to upgrade. These points underscore the conclusion of Giuliani et al. (2005) that "both the local and the global dimensions matter."

3.5.2.3 Industry Clusters as a Road to Human Development

Human development is a broader topic, encompassing multiple areas such as health, economics, and social capital. Amartya Sen summarized it best by saying, "The process of economic development can be seen as a process of expanding the capabilities of people. Ultimately, the process of economic development has to be concerned with what people can or cannot do," (Amartya Sen quoted in Wresch, 2009, p. 262). Hence, to look at the industry cluster strategy as a tool for human development, we must ask what capabilities are expanded by people's involvement in an industry? One well-documented outcome is the educational opportunities within clusters. The shipbuilding, mechanical engineering, and electronics industry clusters in Norway are examples of clusters that capitalize on the educational institutions in their regions to improve their workforce, products, and production (Asheim & Isaksen, 2002). In addition, many clusters such as the ones in the Sinos Valley demonstrate interfirm collaboration to address common needs such as education (Schmitz, 1995). In addition, Schmitz (1995) takes it a step further in claiming a community and regional development component, as mentioned previously. The shared industry knowledge and experiences create social bonds and trust that may have benefits outside of business. Interfirm collaboration also extends to collective action on community and governance issues. Expanding people's social power is a key part of John Friedman's development framework: "development is a process that seeks the empowerment of the households and their individual members through their involvement in socially and politically relevant actions" (Friedmann quoted in Myer, 2011, p. 158).

Hence, if we begin to look at human development through John Friedman's social power framework, we get a mixed picture. Friedmann identifies eight dimensions of social power: "social networks, information for self-development, surplus time, instruments of work and livelihood, social organization, knowledge and skills, defensible life space and financial resources" (Myers, 2011, p. 118). In the examples given in the previous paragraphs, we see industry clusters expand people's social power in the realms of social networks, information for self-development, social organization, and knowledge and skills. However, the remaining four present a mix of criticism and a need for further study. As mentioned in Sect. 3.5.2.1 (economic development), there has been much criticism of the wages and working conditions within industry clusters in "developing" countries (Myers, 2011). Low wages can limit the financial resources, and the required working hours needed to make a living wage can limit surplus time. In addition, Sect. 3.5.2.2 (modernity) touches on innovation in technology, such as tools (instruments) for work (Myers, 2011). Industry clusters are hotbeds for innovation as the concentration of expertise leads to new niche firms.

In Torreon, the researchers highlighted how U.S. partners guarded parts of the industry value chain, specifically the marketing and product design (Bair & Gereffi, 2001). Arguably, these are the creative parts, and the gatekeeping stifles artistic growth and expression from those within the cluster. Further, by imposing U.S. culture in this way, we harken back to the argument from Willis (2011) that while some may see this as development, for others "it is associated with the eradication of cultural practices, the destruction of natural environments, and a decline in the quality of life" (Willis, 2011, p. 3). If individuals in industry clusters outside the United States or Western Europe were involved in the creative process, such as the design of blue jeans in Torreon or shoes in Sinos Valley, what innovations could their unique cultural lenses bring to the products? This question is reminiscent of the points brought forth by Abhijit Banerjee and Esther Duflo, who assert that the "poor" have significant knowledge and reasons for why they do what they do (Myers, 2011, p. 39), which, ironically, is the reason many buyers choose to import products from these clusters, because the enterprises there have a history in their craft that leads to expertise. This was well documented by Schmitz (1995) in the Sinos Valley.

3.5.2.4 Concluding Remarks and Areas for Further Study

As this section has demonstrated, the industry clusters strategy has many opportunities for development purposes. However, this strategy also comes with downsides. The reality is that further study is needed. Most literature on industry clusters focuses on the economic benefits for the firms or nation. However, more research needs to be focused on the individuals in these clusters, as well as the industry cluster's impact on nearby residents. Particularly, it would be interesting to compare the Human Development Index of different industry clusters. Other measures of quality of life, spanning across economic, modern, and human development, should also be examined. Ultimately, differences in culture, geography, economics, and politics will make every industry cluster unique.

References

Allen, T. J. (1977). *Managing the flows of technology: Technology transfer and the dissemination of technological information within the R&D organization*. MIT Press.

Asheim, B. T. (1996). Industrial districts as 'learning regions': A condition for prosperity. *European Planning Studies*, *4*(4), 379–400.

Asheim, B. T., & Isaksen, A. (2002). Regional innovation systems: The integration of local 'sticky' and global 'ubiquitous' knowledge. *Journal of Technology Transfer*, *27*, 77–86.

Audretsch, D. B., & Feldman, M. P. (1996). R&D spillovers and the geography of innovation and production. *American Economic Review*, *86*(3), 630–640.

Bair, J., & Gereffi, G. (2001). Local clusters in global chains: The causes and consequences of export dynamism in Torreon's Blue Jeans industry. *World Development*, *29*(11), 1885–1903.

Breschi, S., & Lissoni, F. (2001). Localised knowledge spillovers vs. innovative milieux: Knowledge "tacitness" reconsidered. *Papers in Regional Science*, *80*, 255–273.

Capello, R. (1999). Spatial transfer of knowledge in high technology milieux: Learning versus collective leaning processes. *Regional Studies*, *33*, 353–365.

Feldman, M. P. (2000). Location and innovation: The new economic geography of innovation, spillovers, and agglomeration. In G. Clark, M. Feldman, & M. Gertler (Eds.), *The oxford handbook of economic geography*. Oxford. Oxford University Press Inc.

Giuliani, E., Pietrobelli, C., & Rabellotti, R. (2005). Upgrading in global value chains: Lessons from Latin American clusters. *World Development*, *33*(4), 549–573.

Gray, M., Golob, E., & Markusen, A. (1996). Big firms, long arms, wide shoulders: The 'hub-and-spoke' industrial district in the Seattle region. *Regional Studies*, *30*(7), 651–666.

Hakanson, L. (2005). Epistemic communities and cluster dynamics: On the role of knowledge in industrial districts. *Industry and Innovation*, *12*(4), 433–463.

Jacobs, J. (1969). *The economy of cities*. Random House.

Jaffe, A. B., Trajtenberg, M., & Henderson, R. (1993). Geographic localization of knowledge spillovers as evidenced by patent citations. *The Quarterly Journal of Economics*, *108*(3), 577–598.

Keeble, D., & Wilkinson, F. (1999). Collective learning and knowledge development in the evolution of regional clusters of high technology SMEs in Europe. *Regional Studies*, *33*(4), 295–303.

Lai, Y. L., Hsu, M. S., Lin, F. J., Chen, Y. M., & Lin, Y. H. (2014). The effects of industry cluster knowledge management on innovation performance. *Journal of Business Research*, *67*, 734–739.

Lawson, C., & Lorenz, E. (1999). Collective learning, tacit knowledge and regional innovative capacity. *Regional Studies*, *33*, 305–317.

Lissoni, F. (2001). Knowledge codification and the geography of innovation: The case of Brescia mechanical cluster. *Research Policy*, *30*, 1479–1500.

Loasby, B. J. (1998). Industrial districts as knowledge communities. In M. Ballet & C. l'Harmet (Eds.), *Industry, space and competition: The contribution of the economists of the past*. Edward Elgar.

Morrison, A. (2008). Gatekeepers of knowledge within industrial districts: Who they are, how they interact. *Regional Studies*, *42*(6), 817–835.

Myers, B. L. (2011). *Walking with the poor principles and practices of transformational development* (Revised ed.) Orbis Books.

Santagata, W. (2002). Cultural districts, property rights and sustainable economic growth. *International Journal of Urban and Regional Research*, *26*(1), 9–23.
Saxenian, A. (1996). *Regional advantage culture and competition in silicon valley and route 128*. Harvard University Press.
Schmitz, H. (1995). Small shoemakers and fordist giants: Tale of a supercluster. *World Development*, *23*(1), 9–28.
Schmitz, H., & Musyck, B. (1994). Industrial districts in Europe: Policy lessons for developing countries? *World Development*, *22*(6), 889–910.
Willis, K. (2011). *Theories and practices of development* (2nd ed.) Routledge.
Wresch, W. (2009). Progress on the global digital divide: An ethical perspective based on Amartya Sen's capabilities model. *Ethics and Information Technology*, *11*(4), 255–263.
Ziemnowicz, C. (2013). Joseph A. Schumpeter and innovation. In Carayannis, E. G. (Eds.), *Encyclopedia of creativity, invention, innovation and entrepreneurship*. Springer.

Chapter 4
Occupational and Skills Clusters

Mark C. White

Abstract Occupational and skills clusters can effectively complement more traditional approaches to traditional industry-based regional analysis. These analytical frameworks often group occupations by shared knowledge, skills, and tasks in ways that highlight regional workforce strengths. As with other analytical frameworks occupational clustering analyses must align with regional priorities, by for instance, focusing the analysis on key labor market segments (e.g., high-tech jobs). These analyses can support multiple user groups such as workforce development agencies, training and postsecondary education providers, and economic development organizations. Moving forward, newer data sources related to real-time labor market information and credential tracking can strengthen and refine these analytical frameworks.

Keywords Occupational clusters · Regional workforce competitiveness · Labor market information · Economic and workforce development · Skills targeting

4.1 Occupational and Skills Clusters Provide a Different Lens for Regional Analysis

Economic development researchers and practitioners commonly use industry cluster analysis—which examines interdependence and specialization within regional economies—to identify regional competitive advantage (Wolman & Hincapie, 2015). Many cluster analyses use interindustry buying and selling patterns to

M. C. White (✉)
Department of Agricultural and Consumer Economics, University of Illinois Urbana-Champaign, Urbana, IL, USA
e-mail: whitemc@illinois.edu

I. Kumar, R. Gallardo (eds.), *Economic Competitiveness*, SpringerBriefs in Regional Science,
https://doi.org/10.1007/978-3-032-20359-5_4

demonstrate the interdependence between firms and regions. However, this approach can prove limiting because these transactional relationships do not reflect other important types of interdependencies (Renski et al., 2007). Most notably, these analyses do not always consider how area workers contribute to regional competitive advantage.

Recognizing the distinction between what businesses make (e.g., motor vehicle manufacturing) and what workers do (e.g., welders) is an important step toward fully understanding a regional economy (Thompson & Thompson, 1987). Measuring the former relies on industry-based employment and wage data (i.e., data organized by North American Industry Classification System (NAICS) codes), while the latter often requires occupational data (i.e., data organized by Standard Occupational Classification (SOC) codes), and these different perspectives can highlight different trends.

Developing analytical methods and tools that provide insights about the geography of talent can further how we understand regional economies. Many industries are mobile, but talent is more place-based. Therefore, economic futures often rely on the regional workforce's inherent knowledge, skills, and abilities. Over the past 20 years, regional researchers have applied the cluster concept to occupations. This approach allows researchers to better understand the relationships, similarities, and dissimilarities among different types of work activities (Feser, 2003). Grouping occupations with similar characteristics such as required education, experience, skills, and common tasks can show what regions do well and how they compare to other regions.

This chapter explores how researchers and practitioners use occupational and skills clusters to better understand the contributions that human capital makes toward regional competitive advantage. It begins by reviewing several notable efforts to operationalize occupational clusters and create regional analytical frameworks. It then highlights how different stakeholder groups can use occupational cluster analysis to inform their economic and workforce development planning and activities. It concludes by identifying several opportunities to further develop occupational cluster analysis to better meet the current and emerging needs for practitioners and researchers.

4.2 Frameworks That Explain Regional Workforce Strengths Remain in Demand

The need for economic development practitioners to understand their local workforce's relative strengths and weaknesses has never been greater. Local workforce capacity can dictate a region's economic opportunities and how that region fits within the broader economy. In an early attempt to understand the relative position of a regional workforce, Thompson and Thompson (1987) identified five distinct regional roles—entrepreneurship, central administration, R&D, precision operation, and routine operation. This framework highlighted the importance of a region's occupational mix in determining its future, because industry employment trends may not reveal the full range of regional activities. Firms in a single industry may locate production in one region and R&D in another, but those activities each require workers with different skills. The versatility and adaptability of the local skill base can also determine the extent to which regions can take advantage of growth opportunities or manage "sunset occupations" lost to automation or globalization.

Feser (2003) created a conceptual framework to identify knowledge-based occupational clusters as a tool to help economic development researchers and practitioners identify the competitive advantages within their regional workforce. This framework relied heavily on two sources—the U.S. Bureau of Labor Statistics (BLS) and the O*Net database. Specifically, the BLS Occupational Employment and Wage Statistics (OEWS) program produces data on occupational employment within a region, and the National Industry-Occupation staffing matrix shows occupational employment within a given industry. The O*Net database provides, among other things, information about the requisite knowledge, skills, education, and experience necessary for individual occupations. Combined, these data can create occupational groups based on the relationships, similarities, and differences among occupations, as well as the relative importance of these requirements to those occupations.

Feser used Ward's hierarchical agglomerative clustering method to subsequently construct a set of 21 knowledge-based occupational clusters. These cluster definitions can inform descriptive and explanatory studies about the geography of human capital when used in conjunction with occupational employment data (e.g., number of jobs, growth, relative concentration, etc.). The subsequent analysis can help economic development practitioners identify targets based on their region's workforce strengths or inform how postsecondary institutions develop programs that better meet regional skill needs.

4.2.1 Occupational Cluster Frameworks Should Align With Regional Priorities

Many subsequent efforts to operationalize occupational clusters used similar data sources and methodologies (e.g., Koo, 2005; Nolan et al., 2011; Slaper, 2014), but those efforts often pursued different goals. For instance, Nolan et al. (2011) prioritized more knowledge-intensive occupations when creating a framework that included 15 knowledge-based occupational clusters. These clusters consisted primarily of occupations that required extensive amounts of knowledge, preparation, and training (i.e., O*Net Job Zones 3 to 5). This framework assumed that knowledge-driven occupations cluster in places with greater innovation potential.

By contrast, Chrisinger et al. (2012) developed cluster definitions that gave greater priority to occupations commonly found in lower-wage, locally serving industries. As a result, their 25 occupational clusters included areas such as personal healthcare and assistance, medical and social assistance, and hospitality and personal services, among others. These clusters provide more insight about many lower-wage occupations by lower-income workers who may possess less formal education and training. This shows that researchers can adapt occupational cluster definitions to target different segments of the workforce and better align with user needs and priorities.

Researchers can also try to appeal to a much broader audience. Slaper (2014), for instance, created a set of 34 different occupational clusters that covered a larger portion of the overall workforce and considered activities covering a wide range of knowledge intensity. For instance, many of the jobs found in Slaper's "Financial, Legal and Inspection Support Services" cluster can be found in the same firms as occupations in his "Financial, Legal, and Real Estate" cluster, but this broader framework allows users to parse out occupations which require relatively less education, training, and experience (e.g., O*Net Job Zones 1 and 2) from those that require greater education and skill. However, Slaper notes that creating a workable set of occupational clusters involves both art and science, and the primary challenge is finding the proper level of aggregation.

Ultimately, effective occupational cluster definitions are sufficiently aggregated to allow users to understand the primary occupational groups within their region, but are also not so specific that they offer no generalizable knowledge. Occupational cluster analysis, or occupationally-focused research more generally, can make important contributions to regional research. Firms within industry clusters—particularly manufacturing-related clusters—often share similar production processes, technologies, and markets, and as a result, they broadly hire workers with similar skill sets (Koo, 2005). Despite this overlap between typical industry clusters and occupational clusters, other forms of interdependence can bind regional economic clusters, and a shared labor pool may only represent one (Renski et al., 2007).

As a result, there remain strong practical reasons to examine clusters from different perspectives. These different perspectives yield insights that may reveal less obvious connections and opportunities. For instance, Markusen and Barbour (2003) noted that knowledge of different materials enabled engineers in Southern California's aerospace industry to find subsequent work in the region's sportswear industry. Similarly, the demand for woodworking skills allowed displaced furniture workers in North Carolina to find work in the state's boatbuilding industry. Consequently, cluster initiatives—large-scale investments and programs that grow and leverage the regional competitive advantage arising from a unique concentration of skills or activities—can change a region's economic trajectory. These initiatives, therefore, can help regional economies transition away from existing clusters losing their relative competitiveness, and instead build more competitive clusters that offer greater future growth potential (Donahue et al., 2018).

4.3 Occupational Cluster Analysis Benefits Multiple User Groups

The responsibility for developing cluster definitions and performing the actual analysis often falls to scholars and consultants, but the resulting workforce analysis can inform the work of economic and workforce development practitioners, employers and corporate decision-makers, and educational leaders (Nolan et al., 2011). As a result, scholars and consultants must not only understand each stakeholder group's information needs, but also effectively translate this information so that it can lead to actionable decisions. This section reviews how occupational cluster analysis can benefit these different user groups.

4.3.1 Workforce Research Informs How Regions Promote Themselves and Build Competitive Advantage

Occupational cluster analysis can inform many core economic development activities including business attraction, retention, and expansion. By understanding their region's intrinsic brain power, education, knowledge, and skills, economic developers can more effectively differentiate how they market their region (Slaper, 2014). Similarly, this analysis can help economic developers learn from—and benchmark themselves to—other regions with a similar occupational mix. Similar labor markets may serve as potential talent pools from which employers can recruit workers, or they may represent competitors for workers with specialized skills and qualifications (White, 2020). If employers offer remote work opportunities, this information can also help inform where they promote those opportunities.

Just as communities target specific industries, so too can they target specific high-growth or knowledge-intensive occupations or occupational clusters (Markusen, 2004). Occupational targeting may include developing customized marketing messages or creating incentives tailored toward industries with a high concentration of specific occupational groups (e.g., engineers, artists, etc.). Ideally, the demand for these occupations would draw from a relatively broad group of industries. Creating regional initiatives that strengthen and invest in local workforce competitiveness is also recognized as a key step in building sustainable regional economic advantage. Investments in training local workers—particularly for more middle-skill occupations—often prove more effective than traditional business incentives because those workers remain, even if companies decide to relocate (Bartik, 2023).

4.3.2 Occupational Clusters Can Inform Targeted Workforce Development Efforts

Beyond economic development, workforce development practitioners can use occupational cluster analysis to address regional challenges tied to declining industries. For example, Kahlaf, Michaud, and Jolley (Khalaf et al., 2021) used a form of occupational clustering to develop occupational transition maps that connected workers from shrinking sectors—such as North Carolina's tobacco manufacturing industry—to more promising careers in growing industries. This method proves especially useful during sudden disruptions like mass layoffs because it bypasses the need for time-consuming and expensive surveys.

Similarly, Khanal et al. (2025) demonstrated how to proactively use occupational data to build a workforce for emerging opportunities—such as the clean energy transition—rather than reactively responding to economic crises. Their work focused on identifying clean energy jobs that could be filled by retraining workers from similar occupations, by using similar cluster principles to solve a specific workforce challenge. This type of analysis clearly benefits workforce transition efforts, but Geel and Backes-Gellner (2011) found that workers transition more easily between jobs within the same occupational cluster rather than between jobs in different clusters. As a result, without employers investing in training and workers becoming more aware and open to opportunities available in different industries, these transitions will not happen naturally.

4.3.3 Occupational Cluster Analysis Can Shape Educational Programming Decisions

Secondary and postsecondary education providers can also benefit from occupational cluster analysis. These institutions regularly receive employer feedback about their needs, but that information is often anecdotal. Although not specific enough to inform detailed course curriculum, this analysis nevertheless can offer both short- and long-term insights into regional workforce dynamics and enable educational leaders to more effectively plan their programs, particularly for those that align with regional economic strengths (Feser, 2003).

In addition, this type of analysis can help institutions better understand the market demand for their educational offerings. By identifying which industries—and specific firms—employ workers in various occupations, education and training providers gain valuable market intelligence that can inform program design and promotion. Jones et al. (2025) demonstrated that integrating systematic labor market analysis, including occupational cluster analysis and curriculum mapping, allowed institutions to more effectively anticipate and respond to the workforce needs of emerging industries such as electric vehicle manufacturing. This information also supports efforts to justify the need and build program demand for new programs—especially those that require substantial capital investment (Donahue et al., 2018).

4.4 New Data Resources and Approaches Can Refine Future Occupational Cluster Analysis

As noted above, many established occupational clustering methods rely on established sources such as the BLS industry–occupation matrices and O*Net occupational skill profiles. Others incorporate additional data sources, such as the U.S. Census Bureau's Public Use Microdata Sample (PUMS), to further examine the relationship between industries and occupations (Currid & Stolarick, 2009; Lin et al., 2019). However, current occupational definitions can prove limiting. Not all occupational definitions keep pace with the changing labor market, as the Standard Occupational Classification (SOC) system only recently added key occupations like "Data Scientists." Consequently, there remains an ongoing need to bolster analytical tools and create new approaches so that practitioners and researchers can answer more specific and contemporary questions.

4.4.1 New Tools and Data Sources Can Advance Occupational Research

Labor market information (LMI) has evolved dramatically over the past decade, and new LMI tools and resources can strengthen our ability to understand occupational and skills clusters. Most notably, several proprietary vendors offer tools that extract and code data elements (e.g., industries, locations, occupations, job titles, required education, skills, certifications, etc.) from online job advertisements. This information is gathered daily (hence "real-time LMI") and therefore provides one advantage over more traditional LMI sources that publish data months or years after the data are collected. These data tools also allow researchers to search for very detailed information about employers, skills, and certification requirements. However, users must recognize several challenges when using these data. Notably, not all industries make extensive use of online job advertisements. Consequently, these data are more useful when the focus is on technology jobs, rather than jobs in agriculture or construction. Moreover, larger firms often post online job advertisements than smaller firms, growing firms are overrepresented, and even though firms may post the same job in multiple places, not all job advertisements are deduplicated (Hershbein & Kahn, 2018).

Despite these limitations, job postings data allow researchers to ask questions that more traditional LMI sources and frameworks for occupational analysis cannot answer. For instance, Bloom et al. (2020) used these data to highlight the types of occupations and skills necessary to support emerging technology areas not covered by the current North American Industry Classification System (NAICS) system. They also allow researchers to refine their analysis by considering factors that make some labor markets unique or cause them to function differently. For example, White (2020) used online job postings data to highlight the skills and qualifications sought by the expanding National Geospatial-Intelligence Agency (NGA) in St. Louis. Specifically, these job postings data showed that NGA needed workers with security clearances and/or government experience. This factor can significantly shrink the potential labor pool because fewer workers possess these qualifications. Filling these positions, therefore, required drawing from St. Louis's existing base of government contractors or attracting workers from other metro areas with similar defense-related workforce needs (e.g., Washington, D.C.; Huntsville, Alabama; Norfolk, Virginia; Colorado Springs, Colorado).

Job postings data has become more prominent over the past 15 years, but data measuring the demand for industry-recognized credentials, certifications, and licenses represent an emerging avenue for advancing occupational analysis and are an area just beginning to garner greater attention in workforce analysis. These credentials better reflect the types of knowledge and skills that employers seek and how many regional workers possess those skills. It might be premature to include this type of information into occupational clustering schemes, but advances are also being made to gather information more systematically about industry-recognized credentials, certifications, and licenses (Credential Engine, 2022). For instance, Renski (2018) used data from the Current Population Survey to show that manufacturing workers with credentials or licenses earn more than those without.

Creating detailed and comprehensive databases about credentials remains a work in progress, but they could potentially help distinguish some of the differences between higher- and lower-skilled jobs within occupations that do not typically require a 4-year degree. As with other data sources, these data come with some limitations. In addition to the current lack of a comprehensive dataset, a recent study from the Georgetown Center on Education and the Workforce found that for 3 out of 10 middle-skill credentials there is little to no direct connection to a specific occupational cluster (Strohl et al., 2024). Although existing sources (e.g., O*Net, BLS OEWS) will remain foundational for occupational research, those sources are not always the most current or detailed. For instance, the O*Net database is continuously updated, but it can take 7 to 8 years to completely refresh that database. As a result, there remains an ongoing need to find effective ways to use these data sources to complement and strengthen existing analytical approaches to occupational and skills clusters.

4.4.2 *Bottom-up Approaches Can Yield Different Insights About Occupational Clusters*

Broad occupational clusters can show the geography of talent across the country, but local and regional efforts often focus more on the workforce needs of firms in specific supply chains (aircraft manufacturing) or market areas (e.g., renewable energy). Markusen's (2004) work on occupational targeting, for instance, showed how this analytical approach could support the arts by building efforts around artistic occupations (e.g., musicians, dancers, actors), more so than performing arts establishments (e.g., symphonies, dance companies, theaters).

Nevertheless, more detailed analysis can lead to more actionable information. For instance, Forbes (2018) used many of the same sources described earlier (e.g., input–output tables, industry–occupation matrices, and occupational skill profiles) to examine the distribution of skills throughout the automotive supply chain, as well as across the different tiers of suppliers. She found that higher-tier suppliers often had workers with greater and more sophisticated manufacturing skills than lower-tier suppliers. Moreover, these skill differentials hindered the ability of lower-tier suppliers to upgrade their processes which could limit the region's ability to expand these activities. Understanding these differences, therefore, can highlight areas that need greater focus and attention.

Broader occupational analysis can provide a top-down view on a region's relative workforce strengths, but regional actors often need more targeted occupational analysis. Rather than considering the regional workforce as a whole, analysts may instead start with an individual occupation and then begin to identify related and similar occupations. This information is already available for jobseekers and counselors. Not only is this information available through the O*Net database, but researchers at the Federal Reserve Bank of Philadelphia created an Occupational Mobility Explorer that allows job seekers to look for occupations in their metro area that require similar knowledge and skills and will pay a higher wage (Demaria et al., 2020).

This bottom-up approach can also prove useful for broader regional analysis. For example, Wong (2011) assigned occupations to the job titles provided in the credits of video games as a way to understand the video game industry's workforce needs. Starting with these key occupations, analysts can begin to look at related occupations and then define an occupational cluster that serves this emerging industry. Once defined, researchers can then place this occupational cluster within the broader geographic distribution of talent and see the other markets that possess workers with similar skill sets.

4.4.3 Effective Occupational Cluster Analysis Must Also Consider Regional Differences

The development of occupational clusters relies heavily on the industry–occupation staffing matrix, but researchers and practitioners must also recognize that these staffing patterns vary among regions (Barbour & Markusen, 2007; Slaper, 2014). Capturing these differences can prove challenging, as BLS only provides national staffing patterns data. State LMI agencies produce industry and occupational employment projections that may better capture the state's economy, but the availability of these resources varies between states. Moreover, these projections may prove most useful when focusing on one state or region but are less useful for broader systematic analysis.

More qualitative research can also help reveal regional differences and uncover the tacit knowledge (Gertler & Vinodrai, 2009; Henry & Pinch, 2000) and untraded independencies (Storper, 1995) that can make regional labor markets unique and competitive. It is these interdependencies—rather than the simple co-location of similar firms or jobs—that make and sustain meaningful clusters. Ultimately, occupational cluster analysis can reveal the geographic patterns of related work activities, but truly understanding how those patterns arose can only come from additional qualitative research.

Moreover, these clusters do not exist in a vacuum, and state and regional priorities and policies can greatly influence how they form and grow. For example, North Carolina built its biotechnology industry by investing in both its innovation ecosystem and workforce training. This enabled the state to develop competitive advantages in both research and biomanufacturing. As a result, North Carolina has created job opportunities for both highly educated workers and workers without 4-year degrees, thereby making progress toward achieving both its innovation and workforce development goals (Lowe & Wolf-Powers, 2018). By contrast, states like Pennsylvania—that have historically been leaders in the pharmaceutical industry—focused their workforce efforts on training high-level scientists and technicians but have not captured the opportunities arising from building both the state's research and manufacturing activities. There is no one way to capture these regional differences, but by combining quantitative and qualitative research, we can more fully understand these regional workforce advantages and what makes them work.

4.5 Conclusions

Examining regional economies through an occupational lens effectively complements more widely used NAICS-based industry cluster approaches. Many occupational cluster schemes utilize the national industry–occupation staffing patterns and information drawn from the O*Net database, but these cluster definitions may vary because different user groups have different needs and priorities. For instance, occupational analysis that informs economic development targeting efforts may emphasize higher-wage jobs in export-oriented industries, but analysis that serves the public workforce system must include information on lower-wage occupations found in more locally serving industries.

Moving forward, the incorporation of new LMI tools and resources will bolster these frameworks. Emerging resources related to online job postings or industry-recognized credentials will allow researchers to ask and answer more specific questions and provide more current information. The responsibility for incorporating these analytical tools and building more robust frameworks falls primarily on researchers, scholars, and consultants. For these resources to be useful, however, researchers must translate this information into products that individual practitioners, employers, or educators easily understand and effectively use to make more data-driven decisions (Khalaf et al., 2021).

References

Barbour, E., & Markusen, A. (2007). Regional occupational and industrial structure: Does one imply the other? *International Regional Science Review*, *30*(1), 72–90. https://doi.org/10.1177/0160017606296727

Bartik, T. (2023). Seize the time: Needed research on local economic development in an era of increased attention to problems of place. *Economic Development Quarterly*, *37*(1), 7–13. https://doi.org/10.1177/08912424221140027

Bloom, N., Hassan, T., Kalyani, A., Lerner, J., & Tahoun, A. (2020). The geography of new technologies. *Institute for New Economic Thinking Working Paper Series*, No. 126. https://doi.org/10.36687/inetwp126

Chrisinger, C. K., Fowler, C. S., & Garshick Kleit, R. (2012). Shared skills: Occupation clusters for poverty alleviation and economic development in the U.S. *Urban Studies*, *49*(15), 3403–3425. https://doi.org/10.1177/0042098011433489

Credential Engine. (2022). *Counting U.S. postsecondary and secondary credentials*. Credential Engine. Accessed from https://credentialengine.org/wp-content/uploads/2023/01/Final-CountingCredentials_2022.pdf

Currid, E., & Stolarick, K. (2009). The occupation—industry mismatch: New trajectories for regional cluster analysis and economic development. *Urban Studies*, *47*(2), 337–362. https://doi.org/10.1177/0042098009349024

Demaria, K., Fee, K., & Wardrip, K. (2020). *Exploring a skills-based approach to occupational mobility*. The Federal Reserve Bank of Philadelphia. Accessed from https://www.philadelphiafed.org/-/media/frbp/assets/community-development/reports/skills-based-mobility.pdf

Donahue, R., Parilla, J., & McDearman, B. (2018). *Rethinking cluster initiatives*. The Brookings Institution Metropolitan Policy Program. Accessed from https://www.brookings.edu/wp-content/uploads/2018/07/201807_Brookings-Metro_Rethinking-Clusters-Initiatives_Full-report-final.pdf

Feser, E. J. (2003). What regions do rather than make: A proposed set of knowledge-based occupation clusters. *Urban Studies*, *40*(10), 1937–1958. https://doi.org/10.1080/0042098032000116059

Forbes, A. (2018). A measure of interdependence: Skill in the supply chain. *Economic Development Quarterly*, *32*(4), 326–340. https://doi.org/10.1177/0891242418791759

Geel, R., & Backes-Gellner, U. (2011). Occupational mobility within and between skill clusters: An empirical analysis based on the skill-weights approach. *Empirical Research in Vocational Education and Training*, *3*(1), 21–38. https://doi.org/10.1007/BF03546496

Gertler, M. S., & Vinodrai, T. (2009). Learning from America? Knowledge flows and industrial practices of German firms in North America. *Economic Geography*, *81*(1), 31–52. https://doi.org/10.1111/j.1944-8287.2005.tb00254

Henry, N., & Pinch, S. (2000). Spatialising knowledge: Placing the knowledge community of motor sport valley. *Geoforum*, *31*(2), 191–208. https://doi.org/10.1016/S0016-7185(99)00038-X

Hershbein, B., & Kahn, L. (2018). Do recessions accelerate routine-biased technological change? Evidence from vacancy postings. *American Economic Review*, *108*(7), 1737–1772. https://doi.org/10.1257/aer.20161570

Jones, G., MacFarland, C., Lee, M., Reid, C., Rose, E., Gottlieb, J., & Falcon, I. (2025). Identifying and developing the battery manufacturing workforce: A regional analysis of supply–demand of skilled workers. *Economic Development Quarterly*, *39*(1), 49–59. https://doi.org/10.1177/08912424241274318

Khalaf, C., Michaud, G., & Jolley, G. J. (2021). How to assess the transferability of worker skills: A hybrid clustering approach. *Journal of Regional Analysis & Policy*, *51*(1), 67–78. https://doi.org/10.22004/ag.econ.339948

Khanal, K., Kaza, N., & Lowe, N. (2025). Occupational transitions into clean energy: A workforce development approach using occupational similarity and unsupervised clustering. *Economic Development Quarterly*, *39*(1), 1–18. https://doi.org/10.1177/08912424251352743

Koo, J. (2005). How to analyze the regional economy with occupation Data. *Economic Development Quarterly*, *19*(4), 356–372. https://doi.org/10.1177/0891242405279910

Lin, T., Stolarick, K., & Sheng, R. (2019). Bridging the gap: Integrated occupational and industrial approach to understand the regional economic advantage. *Sustainability*, *11*(15), 4240. https://doi.org/10.3390/su11154240

Lowe, N. J., & Wolf-Powers, L. (2018). Who works in a working region? Inclusive innovation in the new manufacturing economy. *Regional Studies*, *52*(6), 828–839. https://doi.org/10.1080/00343404.2016.1263386

Markusen, A., & Barbour, E. (2003). *California's occupational advantage* (Working Paper No. 2003.12). Public Policy Institute of California. Accessed from https://www.ppic.org/wp-content/uploads/WP_503AMWP.html

Markusen, A. (2004). Targeting occupations in regional and community economic development. *Journal of the American Planning Association*, *70*(3), 253–268. https://doi.org/10.1080/01944360408976377

Nolan, C., Morrison, E., Kumar, I., Galloway, H., & Cordes, S. (2011). Linking industry and occupation clusters in regional economic development. *Economic Development Quarterly*, *25*(1), 26–35. https://doi.org/10.1177/0891242410386781

Renski, H., Koo, J., & Feser, E. (2007). Differences in labor versus value chain industry clusters: An empirical investigation. *Growth and Change*, *38*(3), 364–395. https://doi.org/10.1111/j.1468-2257.2007.00375

Renski, H. (2018). Estimating the returns to professional certifications and licenses in the U. S. manufacturing sector. *Economic Development Quarterly*, *32*(4), 341–356. https://doi.org/10.1177/0891242418792090

Slaper, T. F. (2014). Clustering occupations. *Indiana Business Review*, *89*(2). Accessed from https://www.ibrc.indiana.edu/ibr/2014/summer/article2.html

Storper, M. (1995). The resurgence of regional economies, ten years later: The region as a nexus of untraded interdependencies. *European Urban and Regional Studies*, *2*(3), 191–221. https://doi.org/10.1177/096977649500200301

Strohl, J., Mabel, Z., & Peltier Campbell, K. (2024). *The great misalignment: Addressing the mismatch between the supply of certificates and associate degrees and the future demand for workers in 565 US labor markets*. Georgetown University Center on Education and the Workforce. Accessed from https://cew.georgetown.edu/wp-content/uploads/cew-the_great_misalignment-fr.pdf

Thompson, W. R., & Thompson, P. R. (1987). National industries and local occupational strengths: The cross-hairs of targeting. *Urban Studies*, *24*(6), 547–560. https://doi.org/10.1080/00420988720080781

White, M. (2020). *Using 'real-time' labor market information to examine the national geospatial-intelligence agency's staffing needs in St. Louis*. Prepared for the Sinquefield Center for Applied Economic Research, Saint Louis University. Accessed from https://www.slu.edu/research/sinquefield-center-for-applied-economic-research/-pdf/nga-bg-draft-with-exec-summary.pdf

Wolman, H., & Hincapie, D. (2015). Clusters and cluster-based development policy. *Economic Development Quarterly*, *29*(2), 135–149. https://doi.org/10.1177/0891242413517136

Wong, H. (2011). *A study of the video game industry in U.S. metropolitan areas using occupational analysis* (Master's thesis, University of Massachusetts, Department of Landscape Architecture and Regional Planning). https://doi.org/10.7275/2207109

Chapter 5
Social Networks

Annie Cruz-Porter

Abstract This chapter examines social network theory and its application to economic cluster development. The analysis traces the evolution of network concepts—including nodes, ties, centrality, clustering, homophily, and structural holes—and connects them to economic geography's relational turn. The analysis demonstrates how social networks conduct knowledge flows, innovation, and social capital formation within industrial clusters. Drawing on studies from Silicon Valley, Chile, Sydney, and the UK, the chapter shows that network structure shapes economic outcomes through coordination, trust, and information exchange. This concludes by introducing social network analysis (SNA) as an underutilized but powerful tool for economic development planning.

Keywords Social capital · Network theory · Social network analysis · Relational economy

5.1 Social Network Theory and Evolution

The prominence of social networks and its theory has emerged strongly since 2000. Social network theory comprises a framework used to study relationships and interactions between individuals, groups, or organizations. It explores how these entities are connected through various types of ties, such as friendships, professional relationships, or communication channels. Some key concepts within social network theory and some of the chief scholars who have consistently advanced

---

A. Cruz-Porter (✉)
Purdue Center for Regional Development, Purdue University, West Lafayette, IN, USA
e-mail: acruzpor@purdue.edu

I. Kumar, R. Gallardo (eds.), *Economic Competitiveness*, SpringerBriefs in Regional Science,
https://doi.org/10.1007/978-3-032-20359-5_5

knowledge in this area include the following (some of whom are cited in this chapter, but not with their seminal work nor as a first author necessarily):

1. Nodes: These are the individual entities within the network, such as people, organizations, or even nations (Granovetter, 2005; Wellman, 2003).
2. Edges (Ties): These represent the relationships or interactions between nodes. Edges can be directed (one-way) or undirected (bidirectional) (Burt, 1992; Granovetter, 2005; Wellman, 2003; Bidart, 2020, and Shalizi & Thomas, 2011).
3. Network Structure: This refers to the overall pattern of connections among nodes in the network. This includes how densely connected the network is, which nodes are central or peripheral, and whether there are clusters or cliques of nodes (Newman, 2006; Borgatti, 2003, 2014).
4. Centrality: This measures the importance or influence of a node within a network. Nodes with high centrality might have more connections, control over information flow, or occupy strategic positions (Freeman, 1979; Bonacich, 1987; Burt, 1992; Faust, 1997).
5. Clustering: This refers to the tendency for nodes to form clusters or groups where nodes within the same cluster are more densely connected to each other than to nodes outside the cluster (Newman, 2006; Girvan & Newman, 2002; and Bidart, 2020).
6. Homophily: The principle that individuals tend to associate with others who are similar to them in characteristics such as age, gender, ethnicity, or interests (Coleman, 1958; Lazarsfeld & Merton, 1954; and Jackson, 2021, 2023).
7. Structural Holes: Refers to gaps between groups of nodes that, when bridged by certain nodes (often called brokers), can provide access to new information or resources (Burt, 1992; Krackhardt, 1999).
8. Small World Phenomenon: This is the observation that in many social networks, any two individuals are connected through a relatively short chain of intermediaries (Milgram, 1967; Strogatz & Watts, 1998).

Social network theory remains primarily interdisciplinary and draws from sociology, mathematics, computer science, and organizational studies. It underpins a wide range of phenomena, from the spread of information and diseases to the dynamics of innovation and collaboration in organizations. An early attempt to elucidate the dynamic and the profuse effects of social networks comes from Malcolm Gladwell's The Tipping Point (2000). He refers to the stickiness of networks needed to attract audience attention and engagement with content. Media that solicits deep audience engagement and aggregates attention (via its networks) to specific content in a centralized place has such stickiness (Cruz-Porter, 2018 and Jenkins et al., 2013). Markusen (1996) uses the term "sticky places" as those that attract and retain capital and labor, despite globalizing tendencies. Stickiness thus influences the retention of knowledge, relationships, innovations, a common pool of resources, and digital transformations to be developed and built via multiple media platforms in specific geographically defined locations with assets that foster the spread of media. Individuals in those areas use their social connections to attract, build, and preserve online reputations that matter greatly in the human capital and labor markets. Sometimes, brief online interactions reflect and/or facilitate this stickiness. It should be noted that stickiness relies on a network to not only support, but also affirm the posting. The entire network does not need to agree or validate the post, but it does require the approval of a set audience to exist.

Social network connections may also be predicted on professional expertise and trust. Thus, professional workforce survival (such as within an industrial cluster) hinges on managing reputation, maintaining knowledge of product or service, and leveraging the social capital accrued from the offline or online social networks. Fenwick (2012: 601) cited McRobbie (2002), who argued that networks are temporary structures based on "fleeting social interaction," not development "through long term collective structure and are linked to personal association and goals of self-promotion and self-advancement," and thereby segregates large portions of the overall workforce from each other (Cruz-Porter, 2018).

Social networks show that relationships rely on people transmitting and sharing content. This, in turn, cascades to others further down the network responding to and possibly augmenting the content before sharing that content in turn (Swani et al., 2014; Ridgeway, 2014). The resulting reciprocity strengthens business relationships and behaviors along a network that are matched to become mutually beneficial over time (Quinton, 2016). Because many professionals are connected via social media with their co-workers (Duggan et al., 2015; Schmidt et al., 2016), this matters significantly to their ability to relate to peers. These ideas will be further explored in this chapter.

5.2 Economic Geography's Relational Turn

While social network theory continued to grow in the 2000s, a relational turn also occurred within the field of economic geography. It became concerned with how networks of firms and production systems vary from place to place. The relational turn sought to increase competitiveness by creating, accessing, and sharing knowledge. The research focused on knowledge sharing beyond global competitiveness, primarily how firms link with one another through knowledge networks can help explain the social organization of individuals. Bathelt et al. (2005) maintain that their theories on the interrelationships of knowledge resources (such as clustered within a sectoral workforce) emphasize the important role of physical infrastructure to ensure competitiveness in a global market. They further assert that global linkages, not local connections, facilitate innovation at technology firms and global knowledge flows. This illustrates that the impact of relational proximities is nuanced and constitutes a significant economic role in society (Tranos & Nijkamp, 2013). Tranos and Nijkamp (2013) outlined several types of proximity which could also pertain to how a network is organized and is, therefore, relational in makeup (Cruz-Porter 2018). Rather, economic activities continue to be based in the physical sense, dependent on infrastructure, geographical proximity, and the organization of people online.

A more theoretical stance on the importance of creating industrial clusters within particular regions and the ways that firms connect with one another in a multitude of complex ways provides a vital part of cluster economic theory. Barthelt and Glucker (2005) explored the "relational turn" in economic geography by exploring the theoretical interactions between resources and how these relationships stimulate effective spatial, technological, and economic development. They identified the following: material resources (such as bundles of services), knowledge, power, and social capital. Each variable works interdependently to influence the success of an economic development project. In terms of regional industries, within a cluster, Bathelt and Glucker (2005: 1553) assert that social relations are "constantly being produced and reproduced through on-going communications between the actors ... about which technologies to use, and the like." They also define social capital on micro- and macrolevels, of which the microlevel constitutes the most important aspect.

This is in part because economic geography underpins their theories on how the interrelationships between resources emphasize the role of physical infrastructures and the different types of resources from a spatial perspective. In addition, these microprocesses highlight the contextual, path-dependent, and contingent nature of economic action and interactions within networks. Bathelt et al. (2005) assert that global linkages, rather than local connections, facilitate innovative performances of tech firms and are pivotal to their ability to innovate.

Overman, Rice, and Venables (2010) applied their economic models to understand new economic geography linkages across regions—a concept dubbed "new regionalism." They found that infrastructure investment or any supply-side improvements produced a "positive productivity shock." This, in turn, impacts the earnings–employment relationships. In terms of technological infrastructure improvements, four relationships (earnings, employment, cost of living, and migration) determine the economic linkages between urban areas. The authors considered these linkages significant to understanding the impacts of policy decisions on neighboring cities and regions. It is unclear whether these findings can be applied on a smaller scale between specific industrial clusters. The implications of applying these theories on a microscale also remain unclear; however, they prefer the application of regional industrial clusters. The empirical evidence that connects industrial clustering with technology innovation in China has also been explored within economic geography.

5.3 Ties, Homophily, and Other Characteristics of Social Networks

Social networks function by leveraging social connections within a structured framework (Cruz-Porter, 2018). Shalizi & Thomas (2011) pointed out that bonded ties form among individuals who are closely situated in a network and possess shared characteristics, exhibit similar behaviors, and experience analogous events.

This raises the question: does this imply a contagion or influential phenomenon, or is it merely a result of the shared similarities among these connected individuals? They argue that various factors contribute to social contagion, including inspiration, imitation, persuasion, biological transmission (such as behaviors prompted by a virus), mutual enthusiasm for certain activities, latent homophily concerning unobserved traits, or an external common cause. Notably, Shalizi and Thomas (2011) observe that homophily and contagion resemble each other so closely that distinguishing between the two can be challenging, if not impossible. Whether one subscribes to the idea of social contagion or homophilic causation, the sphere of influence within social networks is limited to the connections and their relationships. Shalizi and Thomas (2011) propose that this phenomenon may not arise from social contagion, but rather from a series of behavioral choices. Does this effect provide an explanation for social structures, or is the cultural spread merely an adaptation to a newly emerging social framework? These researchers indicate that this dynamic occurs within a homophilic network—either latent or manifest—which creates homogeneous clusters that share specific values. Observationally, it is challenging to make this distinction; even mathematical modeling has struggled to clarify the differences (Shalizi & Thomas, 2011).

5.4 Social Ties, Types, and Design

Connections between individuals are referred to as ties. These ties can also exist between nodes and come in various forms. Research in social network analysis (SNA) has identified three types of ties that are pertinent to social media networks (Kane et al., 2014, p. 282).

Proximities: These are shared physical or social spaces that provide opportunities for tie formation, such as living in the same city and working in the same office (Cruz-Porter, 2018). Proximity can also refer to the organization of a network, indicating its relational nature. The notion that the world is becoming smaller due to easily accessible relationships via smartphones overlooks the complexity of spatial interactions and oversimplifies the idea of place. Economic activities remain rooted in physical settings, relying on infrastructure, geographic location, and the spatial arrangement of people. Traditional economic measures based on industrial production have become outdated and should be replaced with a global framework of flows, which offers an "information-friendly environment" (Stock, 2011, p. 965). Although the roles of knowledge workers, networked cities, and informational cities have been extensively explored, a unified definition in academic discussions is still lacking.

Social relations: These are persistent social connections between nodes, such as friends, colleagues, or bosses. On social media, they represent friends, connections, followers, and affects (likes or dislikes) (Cruz-Porter 2018). Affects, in this case, affirm a relationship node, and because it is not transitory, it sits in the social relation space.

Interactions: These are brief and temporary engagements with another entity, such as conversing face-to-face, sharing a meal, or making a phone call.

All of these may be used to analyze industry clusters further at some point in the future.

5.5 Structure and Relational Flows

Social network structures facilitate movement between money, services, goods, knowledge, information, trust, norms, and sentiments/perceptions. Moreover, the various types of ties—whether representing skills, users, relationships, or content—play a dynamic role in shaping network formation. Granovetter (2005) argues that social structure, represented through social networks, has a significant effect on economic outcomes for three key reasons: first, networks influence both the flow and the quality of knowledge; second, they serve as critical sources of rewards and punishments; and third, trust in others to act appropriately develops within the framework of a social network. The effects of relational proximities are complex and carry substantial economic implications for society (Tranos & Nijkamp, 2013). Knapp et al. (2014) emphasize the importance of relational ties, stating that they shape attitudes, intentions, and behaviors. Their findings suggest that the concepts of fellowship, identity, and psychological ownership are predictors of satisfaction. Nonetheless, the results indicate that identity might not be as crucial for members of the community as initially thought.

The experience of being part of an insider group conveys a sense of fellowship and integration, fostered by various practices and benefits that signal an individual's acceptance as a member. This membership fulfills a basic human desire for connectedness, independence, and influence over one's surroundings. Those who feel included are more likely to take on their responsibilities within the organization, nurturing a positive outlook toward the community, which reflects their emotional commitment. Such individuals are motivated to stay within the community and play an active role in its activities through "innovative behavior."

5.6 Social Capital, Innovation, and Networks

Social capital is intrinsically linked to the idea of networks, emphasizing the significance of relationships (Cruz-Porter, 2018). Bruni and Sugden (2000) contend that the strength of social capital correlates with the density of these networks, as trust, cooperation, and reciprocity enhance the well-being. Bourdieu (1988) defines social capital as "the sum of the actual or potential resources connected to the existence of a lasting network of somewhat institutionalized relationships characterized by mutual acquaintance and recognition." In essence, social capital embodies the obligations and connections that exist among group members. According to Coleman (1990), social capital is regarded as a public good, a collective resource that can be either actual or potential, while Putnam (2000) affirms the significance of relationships among individuals. They observed a notable social transition from nurturing neighborhood connections to focusing on networks primarily comprised of friends and family. Like networks, social capital fundamentally relies on trust and shared understanding. Castells (1996) pointed out that with the rise of a "network society," individuals tend to exchange "bridging social capital" for "bonding social capital" (Hampton and Gupta, 2008), illustrating a noteworthy shift in how social mobility is perceived. While human capital pertains to the inherent qualities and skills possessed by individuals, particularly within the context of the digital economy, social capital typically represents a less tangible resource created through interactions between at least two individuals (White and Green, 2011). Parnwell (2007) presents a conceptual framework for social capital where "associational" social capital emerges from networks, collaborations, interpersonal relationships, and collective endeavors. These collective actions might lead to cultural erosion, increased individualism, atomization, and materialism, while simultaneously diminishing bonding social capital, trust, social engagement, authority, and competitiveness.

For over a century, SNA has been employed within the social sciences to explore the relationships and connections among individuals and their chosen social groups. This approach revolves around networks as its foundational concept, consisting of a series of interconnected dyadic ties. The nodes within these networks can include individual actors, organizations, or elements within the network, with the types of connections characterized as social relationships, such as "friend" or "colleague." Dyadic interactions refer to scenarios where a person "chats" or "promotes" to another. Moreover, a set of ties connects to create paths, which allow nodes to influence one another indirectly. Social network analysis suggests that a node's position within a network structure establishes its opportunities and limitations. Kane et al. (2014, p. 277) point to researchers who have highlighted four key areas within social network studies. These areas include environmental shaping, which examines how the surrounding network affects its members; contagion, which refers to the transmission of resources that influences individuals within the network; structural capital, which focuses on how personal connections can either enable or limit opportunities; and resource access, which concerns how individuals can tap into and benefit from the resources available in the network. Castilla et al. (2000, p. 219) point out that networks in Silicon Valley play a critical role in the labor market, influencing the dynamics of power and the generation of innovation.

According to Castilla et al. (2000), a social network is defined as "a set of nodes or actors (persons or organizations) linked by social relationships or ties of a specified type." Trust among these connections is essential. In their research on social networks in Silicon Valley, they identify two types that impact trust between individuals: relational networks, which shape expectations based on past interactions, and structural networks, which allow individuals to establish connections while minimizing the risk of unethical behavior. Granovetter (2005, p. 36) suggests that "in most real labor markets, social networks play a key role" and characterizes these networks as a form of social capital. He notes that all social interactions involve the exchange of information (i.e., knowledge sharing), which can lead to asymmetric information distribution influenced significantly by social structures. Granovetter (2005) also connects the spread of innovation to social networks, noting that those who are "socially marginal" can more easily diverge from accepted practices since their actions are less constrained by the prevailing norms in closely knit networks. This project aims to explore knowledge-sharing behaviors among three distinct groups by assessing the actions, expectations, and norms of individuals within each cohort.

Granovetter (2005, p. 34) outlines four fundamental principles of social networks that impact economic outcomes. The first principle pertains to norms and network density, explaining that as commonly accepted behaviors become more entrenched, the social network becomes increasingly dense. Higher density facilitates more frequent trust and cohesion among nodes, shaping how information, ideas, and influence circulate. The second principle posits that individuals gain knowledge through their weak social ties, as strong ties often belong to similar social groups and share comparable information. Burt (1992, as noted by Granovetter, 2005) broadened the weak ties discussion by emphasizing how various components of networks should be leveraged to facilitate the flow of knowledge resources across different networks. The third principle highlights the significance of "structural holes," representing individuals in the network who serve as bridges between disparate groups.

Finally, the fourth principle is the interpenetration of economic and noneconomic action, which focuses on how economic and noneconomic activities are socially embedded. Granovetter (2005, p. 36) asserted that "in most real labor markets, social networks play a key role." He calls these networks a form of social capital and states "social interactions inherently serve as conduits for transmitting information and sharing knowledge." This process of knowledge exchange can often result in asymmetric communication, heavily influenced by the surrounding social structure. The variety of experiences within social networks is essential, as demonstrated by Reagans and Zuckerman (2001), who found that R&D teams comprised of diverse social networks achieved higher productivity compared to those connected to more homogenous groups. As noted by Granovetter (2005), weak ties within a network can support individuals by offering diverse connections that contribute to increased social capital. Holgate et al. (2012) examined the impact of social networks within ethnic minority London, UK, neighborhoods in Lambeth and Hackney, where union membership had diminished. Their research revealed that these communities often failed to leverage bridging social capital, resulting in social networks that provided minimal job guidance or support. In fact, the study indicated that reliance on local connections typically limited employment opportunities within ethnic enclaves that largely consisted of familial ties. This insight emphasizes the significance of social networks in relation to employability.

More broadly, social networks serve as a representation of the capacity to forge and sustain social capital (Donald and Blay-Palmer, 2006). Ferrary and Granovetter (2009) discovered that tightly knit social ties cultivated tacit knowledge and fostered an "innovative milieu" for the technology sector in Silicon Valley. They describe Silicon Valley as an area marked by high clustering density, wherein various ties—ethnic, academic, friendly, and professional—play a critical role in knowledge creation (Ferrary and Granovetter, 2009, p. 334). The concepts of clustering density and relationship types are pertinent to industrial innovation. By applying complex network theory to analyze innovation dynamics in Silicon Valley, Ferrary and Granovetter (2009) concluded three key points: (1) Silicon Valley consists of a diverse and interconnected network of agents; (2) the interactions among these agents are multifaceted and self-organizing; and (3) this system is robust enough to resist technological disruptions.

5.7 Network Effects, Dynamism, and Behavior

A notable characteristic of social networks that has emerged in recent years is the concept of "buzz." As defined by the Oxford Living Dictionary (Anon, 2017), buzz refers to being "busy or moving quickly" as well as a "continuous sound." Together, these definitions capture the essence of the urban media landscape. Mould and Joel (2010) view buzz as a crucial concept in creative and cultural industries, particularly at the local scale. Bathelt et al. (2004, p. 38) define buzz as: "specific information and continuous updates of this information intended and unanticipated learning processes, in organized and accidental meetings ... refers to the network of communication and information linkages which develop within a cluster. This occurs in negotiations with local suppliers, in phone calls ... talking to neighbors ... or when having lunch with other employees. The nature of buzz is spontaneous and fluid." Others, such as Grabher (2002), identify "buzz" as an intangible quality often recognized in hindsight.

Social networks thrive on maximizing potential buzz, "noise" (Grabher, 2002), or "project ecologies" (Grabher, 2004) of trends. Mould and Joel (2010) contend that the dynamics of knowledge flows within the advertising sector spotlight the gatekeepers in a highly interconnected industry that embodies the characteristics of the informational city. This is marked by the dominance of the space of flows over the space of places (Cruz-Porter, 2018). The term "space of flows" pertains to the system governing the exchange of information, capital, and power, which shapes the fundamental processes linking societies, economies, and states across various locales (Castells, 1993, p. 136). While Castells' theory lacks a modern example, it can be reasonably applied to several global cities characterized by industrial agglomerations, diverse populations, and skilled workforces interacting in a networked environment. According to Castells, the quintessential cities that define the knowledge economy are characterized by rich information flows that transcend mere geographical considerations, positioning the informational city as superior to the knowledge or creative city. Urban centers emerge as vital nodes within these spaces of flows, facilitating infrastructure development, cognitive networks, concentrated spatial arrangements, and digital links to similar hubs (Castells, 2001). In parallel, the implications of relational proximities are complex, yet they play a crucial economic role in regional and community development contexts (Tranos and Nijkamp, 2013).

Stock (2011) postulates that traditional economic indicators based on industrial output have become outdated, advocating for a new framework focused on a global space of flows that provides an "information-friendly milieu" (Stock, 2011, p. 965). Although the importance of knowledge workers, network cities, and informational cities has been thoroughly examined, an all-encompassing definition remains elusive among scholars. Both the concepts of knowledge society and information society exhibit several common traits: the significance of computers, mobile infrastructure, and communication technologies; the reliance of basic innovations on informational resources; the fundamental necessity of lifelong learning; the constant availability of information and content creation; and the central role of digital information and networks as facilitators. At the core of this assessment is the influence of networks on the dispersal of information, where interactions within a network signify nodal influence. For instance, the concept of network effects elucidates how messages with "pass-along value" and "spreadability" (Jenkins et al., 2013) circulate, prompting questions about their recipients and dissemination methods. Warner (2002) contrasts the media "public" with the traditional idea of an audience, suggesting that the "public" comprises an imagined connection among consumers. This notion crystallizes during moments of recognition when individuals acknowledge their personal stake in circulatory interactions.

5.8 Network Agency

This section highlights some of the economic theories and findings regarding technological development and seeks to illuminate how they may influence economic development at a regional level. Literature regarding technology and economic development strongly favors the theory of clusters and the agglomeration of industrial resources. These concepts appear to fall under the precepts of new economic geography as characterized by Venables (2005). On his view, new economic geography integrates spatial economics and emphasizes the role of spatial clustering in generating specialized industrial activities (Venables, 2005). Several different concepts emerged from the literature gathered which suggest the prevalence, importance, and need for innovative civic infrastructure with technological features to support sustainable economic growth. The following section will discuss some of the relational linkages between media (entertainment industries) and technological infrastructure clusters strategic to economic development.

Jensen (2011) examined the spatial and economic contributions of visual entertainment industries in Sydney and found that government agencies have a strong role in facilitating the siting of creative industry clusters. He distinguished two different types of clusters serving the entertainment field: general and specialized. The specialized media cluster in this case consists of videographers and video game designers, for example. The author did not give a precise or defined category. Jensen (2011) theorized that these clusters formed, in part, because of a shift in greater use of the internet for communications. In addition, Jensen (2011) found that local media productions contributed to the experience of urban places and reinforced the significance of Australian locations. The clustering of media industries "exhibited both regional and local agglomeration forces" (Jensen, 2011, p. 27). Jensen (2011) also questioned whether the clustering models such as network or spatial accurately reflected the Australian entertainment industry. The author speculated that the driving locational factors for entertainment industries throughout the Sydney region were influenced by both regional (generalized) and more specialized cluster dynamics. Jensen (2011) touched on the idea of social networking in Sydney. He explained that networking in virtual settings is, particularly for people in the entertainment field, important because many of these people work alone and need to keep in touch with others in the field. In this sense, location temporarily becomes less important. However, the people needed to have met and networked with colleagues prior to working alone because these networks cannot form within an isolated bubble. The author stated that Sydney clusters "are relatively loose," primarily as the internet allows people to exchange files, video, and communications. Broadband access was a key to business dealings in media industries. (Jensen, 2011). Jensen's findings suggested that the use of technology in these ways eliminates the need for geographic economic clusters. This theory has implications for geographic areas seeking to implement premium broadband services and encourage economic growth.

Cluster development, in Jensen's opinion, remained "embryonic and patchy" within digital industries in Sydney (Jensen, 2011, p. 28). The author also analyzed the relevant industrial infrastructure necessary to support digital industries. Jensen (2011) speculated that the convergence of major media conduits within specified districts (Pyrmont, Redfern, and Australian Technology Park) may shift the concentration of businesses over the long term from the lower north shore to south of Sydney's harbor. The creative ambience (urban villages with quality coffee) of particular places within the entertainment industry becomes central to their ability to connect with other people within their field. Jensen (2011) also noted that media industry strategies varied based on the place within Sydney: Businesses located to the north of the Central Business District (CBD) (Lower North Shore) are more established than those in East Sydney. People working with the entertainment industries experienced intense pressure to become socially connected. This observation linked up to the importance of proximity, interactions, and relations espoused by Stock (2011).

Environmental attributes that support spatial clustering of these industries remain obscure (Jensen, 2011). Jensen (2011) observed that the ambience that attracts successful businesses to a particular area also increases land costs/rentals and hastens to shift cluster patterns to the inner or middle west of the Sydney metro region. In short, the subjects stated that planning should promote the facilitation of networks and clusters rather than interfere with the market.

The concept of "network power" and the ways that gateway locations manifest economic competitiveness are driven by the fact that "networks make possible the creation or the strengthening of interdependencies between places ... it is through networks that territories form a system" (Offner, 2000). This notion refers to all the characteristics of social networks, particularly its ability to influence.

5.9 Role of Networks in Industrial Clusters

Navarro et al. (2009) completed a detailed study on Regional Innovation Systems (RIS) in the European Union (EU) and identified eight important regional groups and policy recommendations. The authors developed 21 indicators based on relational factors such as economic outputs, technological inputs and outputs, agglomeration economies, and social filters. Their findings suggest that innovation-based policies may not be replicated across regions considering the differences in economies, social and locational contexts, and knowledge creation environments. Along similar lines, Truffer (2008) believed that it is fundamental for economic geography to incorporate within the social study of technology.

Liebovitz (2003) analyzed the collaborative processes that supported the economic development of Canada's Technology Triangle. The author highlighted the "institutionalist" view of economic development which places a premium on local innovations. The author argued that institutions play a role in reinforcing norms, routines, and trust between actors and collaborative efforts. It is suggested that the tech triangle thinks and acts like a region "against a history of parochialism where local identities have constituted an important geographical element" (Liebovitz, 2003, p. 2638). The author considers institutionalist perspectives on regional economic development to be inadequate because they neglect the process of institutional change, issues involving diverging opinions, and "undertheorized notions of space and scale." New regional transformations also became the focal point of an evaluation of the alternative hydrogen energy economy in the Teesside, located in the UK (Hodson et al., 2006). In particular, he examined the interrelationships between governance and sociotechnical innovations and the ways that institutions influenced economic transformations. He cited conflictual issues involving the need for regional competitiveness and the need to transform a "historically embedded" disused industrial region into a center of innovation. The hydrogen economy project at Teesside represented a place that could only serve as a test site. Hodson et al. (2006) focused their paper on the struggle to transform the place into a center of innovation excellence despite a climate of obduracy. In doing so, the authors located several issues involving the new regionalist theories including the role competitive pressures played in developing relationships; the role of producing a symbolic narrative based on interrelationships; the failure of the nation-state to communicate the narrative of a reimagined Teesside; and the formulation of institutional decisions predicated on the "attractiveness" and "competitiveness" of the region (Hodson, 2006).

5.10 Network Interactions and Clusters

In Chile, Giuliani (2013) found that regional clusters facilitate the formation of local inter-organizational networks, which act as conduits of (tacit and explicit) knowledge and innovation. Bell and Zaheer (2007) described the ways that social networks serve as a conduit for knowledge which is often rich, fine-grained, and tacit—i.e., "capable of transmitting subtle cues" (Bell and Zaheer, 2007, p. 957). This section will give a precis on knowledge and how it flows within networks. Tacit knowledge consists of experience, competence, commitment, deed, cognitive processes, noncodified elements such as norms, and experiential insights—which cannot be recorded or stored (Nonaka, 1994). It forms the basis of workplace socialization and is therefore pertinent to industrial clusters. On the other hand, explicit knowledge consists of objective, logical and technical information, easily transferable documents, and records (Nonaka, 1994). This includes degrees, certificates, diplomas, and trainings. This type of knowledge is more pertinent to institutional networks which sometimes cross over with industrial networks. Giuliani (2013), however, found that within the Chilean wine clusters the formation of knowledge networks at the microlevel displays the following network characteristics and occurs with the following observations:

- Cohesion effects, which assume that knowledge network growth is characterized by greater cohesion and network closure among firms—a view that coincides with many cluster narratives, but which has not been tested empirically.
- Status effects, which suggest that more prominent firms in terms of their links, tend to reinforce this prominence through the formation of more ties over time, especially relevant in the resource-poor and uncertain contexts that frequently characterize developing/emerging countries.
- Capability effect, which refers to how heterogeneity in firm-level knowledge bases influences the formation of new knowledge ties (Giuliani, 2013; 4–5).

These three effects are driven by various underlying motivations. Cohesion effects lead to more homogenous, egalitarian, and dense networks. Status and capability effects are likely to promote fragmentation and hierarchy within the network structure (Giuliani, 2013). Capability refers primarily to the skills at the firm level and could be viewed from an occupational standpoint.

5.11 The Use of Social Network Analysis (SNA) in Planning and Urban Development

Social network analysis offers planning practitioners and researchers a distinctive approach to understanding complex social dynamics. As Dempwolf and Lyles (2011) explain in their comprehensive review, SNA focuses on relational data—information about relationships between actors—rather than solely on actor attributes like demographics, income, or location. The familiar saying "it's not what you know, but who you know" captures this fundamental distinction: there are two types of knowledge (technical and relational) that require two types of data (attributes and ties).

SNA differs from traditional planning analysis in four key ways (Dempwolf & Lyles, 2011). First, it emphasizes relational rather than attribute data. Second, it requires a different conceptual approach because relationships exist in "relational space"—distinct from physical space. Consider someone far away with whom you communicate regularly via phone or social media. Though physically distant, you maintain a strong relationship. You are distant in physical space but close in relational space. Third, SNA employs different analytical methods. Traditional research uses variable analysis that treats observations as independent, while SNA uses network analysis methods that explicitly acknowledge and measure the interdependence of relationships. Fourth, just as the spatial structure of a region may correlate with actor behaviors and outcomes, the network structure in relational space may also correlate with behaviors and outcomes.

Planners face six types of problems where SNA proves especially useful (Dempwolf & Lyles, 2011). Problems involving coordination, cooperation, and trust are fundamentally relational—they are characteristics of relationships between people, not attributes of individuals. The statement "Actor A is trustworthy" is meaningless without specifying trustworthy to whom. Similarly, coordination only matters when there are multiple actors whose activities need alignment. SNA enables planners to identify structural holes between groups that lack connections, measure bonding versus bridging social capital, visualize trust networks, and assess reciprocity patterns.

Power and influence present another domain where SNA offers unique insights. The concept of "network power" represents "a shared ability of linked agents to alter their environment in ways advantageous to these agents individually and collectively." This shifts from viewing power as something individuals possess to something that emerges from network structure and relationships. SNA can reveal formal versus informal power structures, document power imbalances that undermine equity, help planners assess their own strategic positioning, and identify opportunities for empowerment by finding actors from underrepresented groups who occupy strategic network positions.

Contemporary planning almost always involves coordinating multiple organizations across different scales. Multilevel planning situations can be understood as networks of clusters—subgroups that are densely connected internally but more sparsely connected to each other. Effective multilevel planning requires understanding vertical boundary-spanning (connections between different levels of government), horizontal boundary-spanning (connections across jurisdictions at the same scale), expertise boundary-spanning (connections bringing together different forms of knowledge), and ideological boundary-spanning (connections between groups with different values). SNA provides tools to map the full ecosystem of organizations, identify key bridging organizations, detect coordination gaps, and monitor network evolution.

The distinction between formal hierarchy and informal influence networks is well-established in organizational sociology but often overlooked in planning practice. Formal organization charts show reporting relationships, but they do not reveal who actually consults with whom when making decisions, who has informal influence over key decision-makers, or where communication bottlenecks exist. In communities, informal networks tend to cluster along lines of homophily—similarity in characteristics like neighborhood, ethnicity, socioeconomic status, or issue interests. Planning processes that only engage some clusters may miss important perspectives or create the appearance of consensus that does not reflect broader community views. Planning processes fundamentally involve flows of multiple forms of information between diverse groups. Information flows among planners and between planners and elected officials typically follow established channels, making them relatively efficient. In contrast, information flows between planners and citizens often lack formal structures and face high transaction costs. SNA can identify structural isolation (some groups lacking connections to networks where planning information flows), information gatekeepers (actors who control information flow to others), asymmetric information pathways (information flowing easily in one direction but not reciprocally), and knowledge type mismatches (explicit knowledge flowing through formal channels while tacit knowledge requires strong ties and repeated interactions).

All of these problem types typically treat networks as relatively static—a snapshot at a particular moment. However, networks are fundamentally dynamic, constantly evolving as relationships form, strengthen, weaken, or dissolve. Understanding network dynamics is crucial because urban planning processes themselves change networks by creating new relationships, long-term effectiveness depends on building sustainable networks rather than achieving immediate outcomes, and communities are constantly evolving network structures rather than fixed entities. Network analysis can assess whether relationships persist after planning processes end, track whether previously isolated individuals or organizations become better connected, and identify warning signs like increasing fragmentation or overdependence on individual brokers.

The literature on SNA applications in planning reveals three major themes (Dempwolf & Lyles, 2011). First, studies focusing on community and social capital challenge planners working at multiple scales to engage more precise definitions of "community" and "place." These terms, often used almost synonymously in planning practice, actually describe quite different phenomena. Placemaking creates or enhances physical, social, and symbolic qualities that make a location attractive, while community building creates or strengthens social relationships among people who may or may not be co-located.

Second, applications focused on understanding and improving public participation demonstrate that network structure—not just the number of participants—affects process outcomes, developmental outcomes (whether participants build new relationships and gain capacity), and instrumental outcomes (actual plan decisions). Critically, participants and planners are often unaware of how network structure influences these outcomes. "Pre-plan mapping"—analyzing actor networks before launching participatory processes—can help planners identify which groups are already well-connected, which are isolated, who serves as information brokers, and where structural holes create barriers (Dempwolf & Lyles, 2011).

Third, substantive applications in economic development challenge dominant paradigms. While agglomeration theory emphasizes spatial clustering and knowledge spillovers, network theorists argue that colocation is often a spatial manifestation of underlying network dynamics and that innovation and cluster growth result from multiple overlapping networks rather than proximity alone (Dempwolf & Lyles, 2011). Research comparing knowledge networks (based on patent citations) with alliance networks (based on strategic partnerships) revealed different structural patterns across industrial sectors and between European, U.S., and Japanese firms, suggesting that effective cluster policy must account for these differences. Studies of Silicon Valley found that tightly knit social ties cultivate tacit knowledge sharing, multiple types of ties overlap and reinforce each other, and diverse, interconnected networks create robustness that resists technological disruptions (Dempwolf & Lyles, 2011).

5.12 Conclusions

This section brings together the theoretical foundations of social networks to demonstrate their application to economic cluster development. The connection is fundamental: Both industries and social networks display inherently relational clustering characteristics. Social networks capture how individual economic agents—with their distinct rationalities and strategies—engage in specific patterns of interaction that shape economic outcomes. Understanding these network dynamics is not auxiliary to cluster analysis; it is central to explaining how clusters form, function, and evolve.

Social network analysis offers six distinct problem-solving capabilities highly relevant to planning: analyzing coordination/cooperation/trust, revealing power/influence structures, navigating multiple organizational levels, mapping informal organization, tracing information flows, and tracking network dynamics. These capabilities address challenges that pervade planning at all scales and across all subfields, yet remain difficult to analyze using traditional methods. The applications reviewed—from disentangling community and place to improving participatory processes to understanding innovation networks—demonstrate SNA's unique analytical power. Despite this potential, documented applications remain scarce, limited by gaps in methodological training and research capacity.

The fundamental insight is stark: Planning involves networks of actors, relationships, information flows, and resources as much as it involves spatial patterns, economic trends, or political structures. Yet while planners routinely analyze the latter, they rarely systematically analyze the former. SNA makes invisible network structures visible, transforms tacit relational knowledge into measurable data, and converts intuition about "who knows whom" into actionable strategy. For economic development practitioners seeking to build resilient clusters—particularly in non-agglomeration regions—this analytical gap represents both a critical weakness and a significant opportunity.

References

Anon, (2017). In: 1st ed. [online] Available at: http://www.oxforddictionaries.com/definition/english/buzz

Bathelt, H., & Glucker, J. (2005). Resources in economic geography: From substantive concepts towards a relational perspective. *Environment and Planning A*, *37*, 1545–1563.

Bathelt, H., Malmberg, A., & Maskell, P. (2004). Clusters and knowledge: Local buzz, global pipelines and the process of knowledge creation. *Progress in Human Geography*, *28*(1), 31–56.

Bell, G. G., & Zaheer, A. (2007). Geography, networks, and knowledge flow. *Organization Science*, *18*(6), 955–972. https://doi.org/10.1287/orsc.1070.0308

Bidart, C., Degenne, A., & Grossetti, M. (2020). Living in networks. In *Living in networks: The dynamics of social relations*. Cambridge University Press (Structural Analysis in the Social Sciences).

Bonacich, P. (1987). Power and centrality: A family of measures. *American Journal of Sociology*, *92*(5), 1170–1182.

Borgatti, S. P., & Foster, P. C. (2003). The network paradigm in organizational research: A review and typology. *Journal of Management*, *29*(6), 991–1013.

Bourdieu, P. (1988). *Homo academicus* (P. Collier, Trans.). Polity Press.

Brass, D. J., & Krackhardt, D. (1999). The social capital of twenty-first century leaders. In J. G. Hunt & R. L. Phillips (Eds.), *Out-of-the-box leadership* (pp. 179–194).

Bruni, L., & Sugden, R. (2000). Moral canals: Trust and social capital in the work of Hume, Smith and Genovesi. *Economics and Philosophy*, *16*(1), 21–45.

Burt, R. (1992). *Structural holes: The social structure of competition*. Harvard University Press.

Castells, M. (1993). The informational economy and the new international division of labor. In *The new global economy in the information age* (pp. 15–43). Macmillan Education UK.

Castells, M. (1996). The information age: Economy, society, and culture. Volume I: The rise of the network society.

Castells, M. (2001). Space of flows, space of places: Materials for a theory of urbanism in the information age. In *The city reader* (pp. 572–582).

Castilla, E. J., Hwang, H., Granovetter, E., & Granovetter, M. (2000). Social networks in Silicon Valley. In M. Kenney (Ed.), *Understanding Silicon Valley: The anatomy of an entrepreneurial region* (pp. 218–247). Stanford University Press.

Coleman, J. (1958). Relational analysis: The study of social organizations with survey methods. *Human Organization*, *17*, 28–36.

Coleman, J. S. (1990). Foundations of social capital. *Cambridge: Belknap.*

Cruz-Porter, A. (2018). *In pursuit of recognition in a digitally divided city: Conceptualizing voice, visibility and presence in the age of social media*. Ph.D. thesis, University of Sheffield. Available at https://etheses.whiterose.ac.uk/21181/.

Dempwolf, C. S., & Lyles, L. W. (2011). The uses of social network analysis in planning: A review of the literature. *Journal of Planning Literature*, *27*(1), 3–21. Original work published 2012. https://doi.org/10.1177/0885412211411092.

Donald, B., & Blay-Palmer, A. (2006). The urban creative-food economy: Producing food for the urban elite or social inclusion opportunity? *Environment and Planning A*, *38*(10), 1901–1920.

Duggan, M., Ellison, N. B., Lampe, C., Lenhart, A., & Madden, M. (2015). *Social media update 2014*. Pew Research Center.

Faust, K. (1997). Centrality in affiliation networks. *Social Networks*, *19*(2), 157–191.

Fenwick, T. (2012). Negotiating networks of self-employed work strategies of minority ethnic contractors. *Urban Studies*, *49*(3), 595–612.

Ferrary, M., & Granovetter, M. (2009). The role of venture capital firms in Silicon Valley's complex innovation network. *Economy and Society*, *38*(2), 326–359.

Freeman, L. C. (1979). Centrality in social networks conceptual clarification. *Social Networks*, *1*, 215–239.

Girvan, M., & Newman, M. E. (2002). Community structure in social and biological networks. *Proceedings of the National Academy of Sciences, 99*(12), 7821–7826.

Giuliani, E. (2013). Network dynamics in regional clusters: Evidence from Chile. *Research Policy, 42*(8), 1406–1419.

Gladwell, M. (2000). *The tipping point: How little things can make a big difference*. Little, Brown and Company.

Grabher, G. (2002). Fragile sector, robust practice: Project ecologies in new media. *Environment and Planning A, 34*, 1911–1926.

Grabher, G. (2004). Learning in projects, remembering in networks? Communality, sociality, and connectivity in project ecologies. *European Urban and Regional Studies, 11*(2), 103–123.

Granovetter, M. (2005). The impact of social structure on economic outcomes. *Journal of Economic Perspectives, 19*(1), 33–50.

Hampton, K. N., & Gupta, N. (2008). Community and social interaction in the wireless city: Wi-Fi use in public and semi-public spaces. *New Media and Society, 10*(6), 831–850.

Hodson, M., & Marvin, S. (2006). Policy IV: Regional science in action in Teesside. *Regions Magazine, 263*(1), 13–14. https://doi.org/10.1080/780346873

Holgate, J., Pollert, A., Keles, J., & Kumarappan, L. (2012). Union decline and voice among minority ethnic workers: Do community-based social networks help to fill the gap? *Urban Studies, 49*(3), 613–630.

Jackson, M. O. (2021, March 20). *Inequality's economic and social roots: The role of social networks and homophily*.

Jackson, M. O., Nei, S., Snowberg, E., & Yariv, L. (2023). *The dynamics of networks and homophily*. CESifo Working Paper No. 10210.

Jenkins, H., Ford, S., & Green, J. (2013). *Spreadable media: Creating value and meaning in a networked culture*. New York University Press.

Jensen, R. (2011). The spatial and economic contribution of Sydney's visual entertainment industries. *Australian Planner, 48*(1), 24–36.

Kane, G. C., Alavi, M., Labianca, G., & Borgatti, S. P. (2014). What's different about social media networks?: A Framework and research agenda. *MIS Quarterly, 38*(1), 275–304.

Knapp, M. L., Vangelisti, A. L., & Caughlin, J. P. (2014). *Interpersonal communication & human relationships*. Pearson Higher Ed.

Lazarsfeld, P., & Merton, R. K. (1954). Friendship as a social process: A substantive and methodological analysis. In M. Berger, T. Abel, & H. Charles (Eds.), *Freedom and control in modern society*. Van Nostrand.

Markusen, R. (1996). Politics of intervention in design: Feminist reflections on the Scandinavian tradition. *AI and Society, 10*(2), 127–141.

McRobbie, A. (2002). From holloway to hollywood: Happiness at work in the new cultural economy. In Paul du Gay & Michael Pryke (Eds.), *Cultural economy: Cultural analysis and commercial life* (pp. 97–114). Sage.

Mehra, A., Borgatti, S. P., Soltis, S., Floyd, T., Ofem, B., Halgin, D. S., & Kidwell, V. (2014). Imaginary worlds: Using visual network scales to capture perceptions of social networks. In D. J. Brass, G. Labianca, A. Mehra, D. S. Halgin, & S. P. Borgatti (Eds.), *Research in the sociology of organizations* (Vol. 40). Emerald Publishing.

Milgram, S. (1967). The small world problem. *Psychology Today, 2*, 60–67.

Mould, O., & Joel, S. (2010). Knowledge networks of 'buzz' in London's advertising industry: A social network analysis approach. *Area, 42*(3), 281–292.

Navarro, M., Gibaja, J. J., Bilbao-Osorio, B., & Aguado, R. (2009). Patterns of innovation in the EU-25 regions: A typology and policy recommendations. *Environment and Planning C: Government and Policy, 27*, 815–840.

Newman, M., Barabási, A. L., & Watts, D. J. (Eds.). (2006). *The structure and dynamics of networks*. Princeton University Press.

Nonaka, I. (1994). A dynamic theory of organizational knowledge creation. *Organization Science, 5*(1), 14–37.

Offner, J. M. (2000). 'Territorial deregulation': Local authorities at risk from technical networks. *International Journal of Urban and Regional Research, 24*, 165–182.
Overman, H., Rice, P., & Venables, A. (2010). Economic linkages across space. *Regional Studies, 44*(1), 17–33.
Parnwell, M. J. (2007). Neolocalism and renascent social capital in northeast Thailand. *Environment and Planning D: Society and Space, 25*(6), 990–1014.
Putnam, R. D. (2000). Bowling alone: America's declining social capital. In L. Crothers & C. Lockhart (Eds.),*Culture and politics* (pp. 223–234). Palgrave Macmillan.
Quinton, S., & Wilson, D. (2016). Tensions and ties in social media networks: Towards a model of understanding business relationship development and business performance enhancement through the use of LinkedIn. *Industrial Marketing Management, 54*, 15–24. https://doi.org/10.1016/j.indmarman.2015.12.001
Reagans, R., & Zuckerman, E. W. (2001). Networks, diversity, and productivity: The social capital of corporate R&D teams. *Organization Science, 12*(4), 502–517.
Ridgeway, C. (2014). Why status matters for inequality. *American Sociological Review, 79*(1), 1–16. Available at. https://doi.org/10.1177/0003122413515997
Schmidt, A. M., Leichook, M., & James, E. (2016). The relationship between social media co-worker connections and work-related attitudes. *Computers in Human Behavior, 55*, 439–445.
Shalizi, C. R., & Thomas, A. C. (2011). Homophily and contagion are generically confounded in observational social network studies. *Sociological Methods and Research, 40*(2), 211–239.
Stock, W. G. (2011). Informational cities: Analysis and construction of cities in the knowledge society. *Journal of the Association for Information Science and Technology, 62*(5), 963–986.
Strogatz, S. H., & Watts, D. J. (1998). Collective dynamics of small world networks. *Nature, 393*, 440–442.
Swani, K. (2014). *What messages to post?: Evaluating the effectiveness of social media communications based on market and offering characteristics* (Doctoral dissertation, University of Massachusetts Amherst).
Tranos, E., & Nijkamp, P. (2013). The death of distance revisited: Cyber-place, physical and relational proximities. *Journal of Regional Science, 53*(5), 855–873.
Truffer, B. (2008). Society, technology, and region: Contributions from the social study of technology to economic geography. *Environment and Planning A, 40*(4), 966–985.
Venables, A. (2005). Spatial disparities in developing countries: Cities, regions, and international trade. *Journal of Economic Geography, 5*(1), 3–21.
Warner, M. (2002). Publics and counter publics. *Public Culture, 14*(1), 49–90.
Wellman, B., Quan-Haase, A., Boase, J., Chen, W., Hampton, K., Díaz, I., & Miyata, K. (2003). The social affordances of the Internet for networked individualism. *Journal of Computer-Mediated Communication, 8*(3).
White, R. J., & Green, A. E. (2011). Opening up or closing down opportunities?: The role of social networks and attachment to place in informing young peoples' attitudes and access to training and employment. *Urban Studies, 48*(1), 41–60.

The manufacturer's authorised representative in the EU is Springer Nature Customer Service Centre GmbH, Europaplatz 3, 69115 Heidelberg, Germany. If you have any concerns regarding our products, please contact ProductSafety@springernature.com

Printed and bound by CPI Group (UK) Ltd, Croydon, CR0 4YY
07/10/2026
02229363-0001